CCCC STUDIES IN WRITING & RHETORIC

Edited by Victor Villanueva, Washington State University

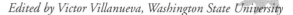

The aim of the CCCC Studies in Writing & Rhetoric Series is to influence how we think about language in action and especially how writing gets taught at the college level. The methods of studies vary from the critical to historical to linguistic to ethnographic, and their authors draw on work in various fields that inform composition—including rhetoric, communication, education, discourse analysis, psychology, cultural studies, and literature. Their focuses are similarly diverse—ranging from individual writers and teachers, to work on classrooms and communities and curricula, to analyses of the social, political, and material contexts of writing and its teaching.

SWR was one of the first scholarly book series to focus on the teaching of writing. It was established in 1980 by the Conference on College Composition and Communication (CCCC) in order to promote research in the emerging field of writing studies. As our field has grown, the research sponsored by SWR has continued to articulate the commitment of CCCC to supporting the work of writing teachers as reflective practitioners and intellectuals.

We are eager to identify influential work in writing and rhetoric as it emerges. We thus ask authors to send us project proposals that clearly situate their work in the field and show how they aim to redirect our ongoing conversations about writing and its teaching. Proposals should include an overview of the project, a brief annotated table of contents, and a sample chapter. They should not exceed 10,000 words.

To submit a proposal, please register as an author at www.editorial manager.com/nctebp. Once registered, follow the steps to submit a proposal (be sure to choose SWR Book Proposal from the drop-down list of article submission types).

D0879999

FREEDOM WRITING

AFRICAN AMERICAN CIVIL RIGHTS LITERACY ACTIVISM, 1955–1967

Rhea Estelle Lathan
Florida State University

Conference on College Composition and Communication

National Council of Teachers of English

Staff Editor: Bonny Graham
Series Editor: Victor Villanueva
Interior Design: Mary Rohrer
Cover Design: Mary Rohrer and Lynn Weckhorst

NCTE Stock Number: 17880; eStock Number: 17897
ISBN 978-0-8141-1788-0; eISBN 978-0-8141-1789-7

It is the policy of NCTE in its journals and other publications to provide a forum for the open discussion of ideas concerning the content and the teaching of English and the language arts. Publicity accorded to any particular point of view does not imply endorsement by the Executive Committee, the Board of Directors, or the membership at large, except in announcements of policy, where such endorsement is clearly specified.

Every effort has been made to provide current URLs and email addresses, but because of the rapidly changing nature of the Web, some sites and addresses may no longer be accessible.

Publication partially funded by a subvention grant from the Conference on College Composition and Communication of the National Council of Teachers of English.

Library of Congress Cataloging-in-Publication Data
Lathan, Rhea Estelle, 1961-
    Freedom writing: African American civil rights literacy activism, 1955-1967 / Rhea Estelle Lathan, Florida State University.
        pages cm. — (CCCC studies in writing & rhetoric)
    Includes bibliographical references and index.
    ISBN 978-0-8141-1788-0 ((pbk.))
    1. Literacy—Social aspects—United States—History—20th century. 2. Literacy programs—United States—History—20th century. 3. African Americans—Education—Social aspects. 4. African Americans—Civil rights—History—20th century. 5. Civil rights movements—United States—History—20th century. I. Title.
    LC151.L26 2015
    302.2'2440973—dc23
                                                                    2015018284

CONTENTS

ACKNOWLEDGMENTS

FREEDOM WRITING WAS BORN OUT OF AMAZING GRACE: unearned, unmerited favor. I'm aware that I've been allowed to do this work due to the remarkable generosity and sacrifices of many people. Ultimately, I owe my gratitude to Civil Rights activists—seen and unseen—editors, scholars, students, friends, family, and my Creator. The National Center on English Learning and Achievement, the Woodrow Wilson National Fellowship Foundation, and the University of Wisconsin's Literacy and Opportunity Fund provided support as I carried this research forward. I wish to thank the library archivists at Avery Research Center in Charleston, South Carolina; the Highlander Research and Education Center in New Market, Tennessee; and the Martin Luther King, Jr. Center for Nonviolent Social Change in Atlanta, Georgia.

I hold immense appreciation for Victor Villanueva, Studies in Writing and Rhetoric Series editor and my real-life intellectual godfather. Victor immediately saw the possibilities and promise of this project and has skillfully ministered me through the publication process. His lifelong commitment to racial justice, human rights, and the freedom struggle is an inspiration to all young scholars doing this work. Not only has he taught me how to be a better writer, but he also inspires me to be a better scholar activist. I'm incredibly blessed and grateful for his approval and favor.

Thank you to the National Council of Teachers of English/Conference on College Composition and Communication (NCTE/ CCCC) Black Caucus members who have nourished my thinking, inviting me to present versions of this book at conferences. I appreciate those who read conference drafts, including David Holmes, David Kirkland, Ersula Ore, Staci Perriman-Clark, Tonya Perry, and Gwen Pough, Within CCCC, a remarkable circle of scholars has nourished my thinking: Julie Nelson Christoph, Beth Daniell, Jenn Fishman, Lynée Lewis Gaillet, Eli Goldblatt, Keith Miller, Peter Mortenson, Rebecca S. Nowacek, and Morris Young. I appreciate every teacher and colleague who has engaged with me in reciprocal learning because every encounter has enriched my compassion and strengthened my resilience. Many thanks to Michael Bernard-Donals, Kristie Fleckenstein, David Flemming, Tarez Graban, Jerrilyn McGregory, Maxine Montgomery, Michael Neal, Martin Nystrand, Malea Powell, and Candace Ward.

For all their helpful comments on drafts, I am deeply indebted to my writing partners as well as the people who read various versions along the way and offered immensely valuable suggestions. Thanks to Ellen Cushman, Alesha Gaines, David Ikard, Stephanie Kerschbaum, Terese Monberg, Eric Pritchard, and Charles Radcliffe. I am fortunate, as well, in the meticulous eye of Bonny Graham, whose useful suggestions and impeccable copyediting did much to improve the manuscript's flow. I appreciate your patience and encouragement. To my Smitherman/Villanueva Summer Writing Collective: Steven Alvarez, Bill Endres, Frank David Green, Aja Martinez, Roxanne Mountford, Gabriela Rios, and Nazera Wright.

I have benefited from the generosity and guiding favor of exceptional academicians who invested immeasurable personal and professional resources in my training, including Deborah Brandt, Keith Gilyard, Stanlie James, Gloria Ladson-Billings, Shirley Wilson Logan, Jacquline Jones Royster, Timothy B. Tyson, and Craig Werner. I have been able to do this work largely because of the mentoring of these scholars, combined with institutional supports. I also appreciate Beverly Moss for reminding me to stay on task amidst the never-ending barrage of potential distractions, and Adam Banks, Adrienne Dixson, Carmen Kynard, and Tamekia Carey (my friend) for providing wonderful distractions. I acknowledge the enthusiasm of my graduate students Janelle Jennings Alexander, Yumani Davis, Yolanda Franklin, Jenise Hudson, Kendra Mitchell, Janeen Price, Esther Spencer, and Cocoa Williams, as well as Dr. Bonnie Jean Williams, all of whom continually renewed my own interest in the importance of this work. I count these women among my many blessings in this life.

My beloved community is made up of some of the best folks around. They have enriched my life in innumerable ways. Thank you Ronda DeShields, Delores and Major Ealey (Bull and Tree), and Teresa Hamm. At least a lifetime of relationships and opportunities has contributed to this book. Gratitude flows to each person who has shared with me in any way, who has fed or befriended me; taught or challenged me; supported or mentored me; mended, forgiven, or inspired me; or been open to receiving these gifts from me. More thanks to Nellie Y. McKay, Elaine Richardson, and Geneva Smitherman for every opportunity you have given me to learn and expand my understanding and for every moment of compassion and happiness you have shared with me.

I am most grateful to my family. To my parents, Ray and Norma Lathan, who raised me to look back but not stare. To my Aunt Shirley and Uncle Henry, who taught me how to pray: my most valuable literacy lesson. Thank you. I'm grateful to my Aunt Denise Morris; my brothers, Ira Lathan, Robert (R. M.) Lathan, and Saladin McIntosh; and my sisters, Letitia and Samara McIntosh, for keeping me in the race. I offer special appreciation to Odessa Johnson Madlock, my "Nana," and Dr. Elvira J. Morris, my "Sugarlump," and my godparents, Drs. Joseph and Connie Sims, who taught me to look past the dark days of discouragement and defeat to realize my full potential. To my extraordinary children, Carla Denise Lathan and Cordale Anthony Rowe, and grandson, Dayshaun Anthony Rowe, thanks for giving me a chance to be your mother and Nonnie; your love, compassion, and wisdom inspire me in all ways. I submit this book as an offering to you and future generations. May it inspire you to create untold legacies of compassion and action. Martha, thank you for the breath of life.

This journey would not have been possible without my Hope. I owe my deepest gratitude and appreciation to my dear wife. Thank you for reminding me that chicken is not a vegetable and for being the prayer police in our home. Thank you for listening to me talk about this project, pretending to understand literacy theory, and learning to drive in the snow. Most of all, thank you for helping me remember who I am and whose I am. Thank you for the Journey— the Journey continues.

So at last, here it is. Ultimately this book honors nine members of Emanuel African Methodist Episcopal Church in Charleston, South Carolina. *But for the Amazing Grace of the Creator . . .*

INTRODUCTION: THE GOSPEL ACCORDING TO LITERACY

Paul and Silas, bound in jail
Had no money for to go their bail
Keep your eyes on the prize, hold
Hold on (hold on), hold on (hold
on)
Paul and Silas began to shout
The jail door opened and they
walked out
Keep your eyes on the prize, hold
on

Freedom's name is mighty sweet,
soon one day we're gonna meet.

Got my hand on the Gospel plow,
I wouldn't take nothing for my
Journey now.

The only chain that a man can
stand,
is that chain of hand and hand.

The only thing we did wrong,
stayed in the wilderness a day too
long.
Keep your eyes on the prize, hold on
Alice Wine

There was also a new bidding—and we could feel it from the vantage point of our Citizenship Program—across class and educational lines, across generations, across localities and dialects and family backgrounds. We could hear this unity in the singing voices and speaking voices of the people; it seemed we could even hear it in the earth itself, like a soft rumbling, a rhythmic beating of drums from all over the South. It was knowing, with undeniable and unshakable conviction, that our time had come.

Andrew Young, *An Easy Burden*

THE SOUTH CAROLINA CITIZENSHIP SCHOOL fairytale goes something like this: Once Upon a Time, in the South Carolina swamps, Septima Clark, a matronly schoolteacher, gathered a few tired, illiterate farmers and taught them to read and write. This bunch of tattered Jim Crow shuckin' Lowcountry residents, suddenly, with little forethought, decided they wanted social equality. With Clark's help, they learned how to read the South Carolina Constitution. Armed with their newly acquired "literacy," the farmers fearlessly marched into the Charleston City Hall and, magically, without incident, registered as voters. Literacy saved the day. Literacy was the golden key that unlocked the gates to civic freedom. White South Carolinians surrendered their Jim Crow practices, integrated lunch counters, and graciously opened schools to black children.[1] The fairytale ends as Septima Clark runs the notorious Jim Crow laws out of South Carolina. And the South Carolina Sea Islands residents lived happily ever after. The End.

This is a nice, neat fantasy. Other romantic adaptations have Clark traveling all over the South with a bag of literacy, which she spreads like pixie dust over "Jim Crow," leading to his ultimate demise. These romantic adaptations reinforce an African American rags-to-riches fantasy that ultimately perpetuates misrepresentations of African American literacy activism. They also legitimize social inequalities that stem from uncritical and incomplete histories. When we tell the stories of our leaders in the struggle for our rights, rarely do we look beyond "Super Septima," "Tired Rosa Parks," or "Mighty Man-on-the-Mountain Martin Luther King Jr." We don't have to look far to locate nostalgic movies or documentary films about the brave Freedom Riders, courageous Montgomery bus boycotters, or heroic Selma marchers. However, if we consider civil rights icon Andrew Young's declaration from the vantage point of the Citizenship Program, we hear an instrument that amplifies local, community-based voices. A more complete narrative restores participant voices to the historical record. This occurs when we listen carefully to the people dedicated to both teaching and learning.[2]

An oversimplified narrative of the Civil Rights Movement in general, or an uncritical analysis of the Citizenship Schools specifically, casts a shadow on primary sources of African American literacy practices. *Freedom Writing* illuminates principal resources and lays bare the Citizenship Schools myth, which is often a placatory narrative that obscures hard truths about the role of writing—learning and teaching—during the Civil Rights era. Literacy activism is especially viable within the context of a social movement designed to take up the ongoing fight against intellectual oppression.

The Citizenship Schools are a chapter in the continuing struggle against the overwhelming justification for relegating black people to subhuman positions: the belief that they were, by and large, illiterate. Not until the 1954 *Brown v. Board of Education of Topeka* decision did we begin to see the demise of prevailing US education policies that had enforced laws preserving educational access exclusively for whites (Prendergast, *Literacy* 16). The decision emboldened black communities en masse to demand their inalienable constitutional rights. The *Brown* decision was the gateway to civic inclusion, but Citizenship Schools were the path up to the door.

Beginning with fourteen students on Johns Island, South Carolina, the schools grew to include more than 60,000 participants throughout the South and later became the largest program of Martin Luther King Jr.'s Southern Christian Leadership Conference (SCLC). The schools set a precedent in mass literacy activity for African Americans that extended far beyond the goal of African American voter registration. They were an empowering force against the dehumanizing strain of segregationist ideologies, guiding many participants into activism. Then, as now, national studies claimed that African Americans lacked the literacy skills required to keep pace with their white American counterparts. If we look to the Citizenship Schools for an innovative perspective on literacy, we both recover and revise a vocabulary for discussing the literacy history of marginalized groups—in this case, the learners and teachers who participated in the Civil Rights crusade.

KEEP YOUR EYES ON THE PRIZE: A REVISIONIST PERSPECTIVE

A revisionist narrative of the Citizenship Schools could begin something like this: In 1954, Alice Wine, a domestic and factory worker, memorized the necessary sections of the South Carolina Constitution in order to pass a voter registration literacy test. Cognizant of the consequences that came with resisting Jim Crow protocol, Wine walked into the voter registration office on Society Street in

Charleston and, invoking a calculated mnemonic strategy, recited the appropriate passage. Wine proudly described her intellectual manipulation, explaining: "'Everybody had to read and get a paper, read and get a paper. . . . And then the man put me for read, and I read those things just like I been know 'em. And I didn't know them things, I swear!'" (qtd. in Carawan and Carawan, *Ain't You Got*).[3] Wine's unrestricted courage, motivation, determination, and ultimately successful registration empowered a Johns Island businessman and community activist, Esau Jenkins, to initiate funding efforts for an adult literacy program.

Jenkins operated a bus service transporting workers between the Sea Islands and Charleston. As a passenger on his bus, Wine bargained with Jenkins that if he taught her to read during those long rides to Charleston, she would take the voter registration literacy test. Both found the process more challenging than anticipated, so memorization became the immediate solution. Jenkins had very little faith in the memorization tactic and didn't think Wine would pass the test. Wine, however, remained determined. She passed the literacy test and received her voter registration certificate. Jenkins explained that Wine's resolve to learn was his ultimate motivation as he set out to solicit funding for a Sea Islands adult literacy program. In 1956, Alice Wine became one of the first participants in the Citizenship Education Program on Johns Island, South Carolina.

But just as the African American fight for civic inclusion did not begin on a bus in Alabama, Alice Wine's activism did not begin on a bus in South Carolina. In 1945, Wine participated in the strike of the Negro Food and Tobacco Workers Union of Charleston. During this strike, she revised a Negro spiritual into a protest anthem. Most people recognize "Hands on the Plow" as a Civil Rights anthem, but few people know it was Alice Wine who revised the lyrics. The Student Nonviolent Coordinating Committee (SNCC) Freedom Riders sang this song while they were literally "bound in jail." They sang as they endured brutal beatings and undue prosecution and imprisonment in Mississippi's notorious Parchman Farm (Mississippi State Penitentiary). Freedom Rider and Congressman John

Lewis explains that the lyrics "Hold on Hold on . . . encouraged us to go on in spite of it all" (Guttentag and Sturman). The lyrics were shouted and moaned in the midst of almost every Civil Rights protest from the 1950s on.

Singing was one of the creative rhetorical strategies adopted by Civil Rights activists to protest segregation. The various strategies drew heavily on the black church, which provided sanctuary for protest rallies and a venue to plan resistance tactics. Despite the centrality of songs in black social justice protest, however, we have yet to account for their rhetorical appeal or literate power, particularly as a way of knowing. In 1942, Zora Neale Hurston introduced the idea of complicating perceptions about African American spiritual expressions, framing them as a theoretical concept: "The real spirituals are not really just songs. They are unceasing variations around a theme" (869). Hurston warns us not to reduce African American compositions of expression to rote performance because these activities are taken up with deliberate attention to a history. Engaging Hurston's gaze, we can see how Alice Wine and other African American freedom crusaders combined song with their liberatory activities and how musical ideologies were an intricate source of black activism. Keith Gilyard expands this theory, arguing that African American rhetorical strategies, along with sacred activities, are crucial components in African American discourse ("Introduction").[4] From this perspective, we can consider how Alice Wine and other African American activists combined sacred language with secular liberatory activities. An example of this relationship is the way that Citizenship School participants replicated religious services while learning, following the format of basic church services: devotion, sermon, and benediction. The devotional service includes a scripture reading and a series of call-and-response songs followed by a prayer and members testifying or witnessing about an overwhelming or extremely difficult situation. The sermon begins with another reading from the sacred text—often the Bible—and a statement of the sermon's theme. The preacher teaches the "Word." Finally, the benediction sends the congregation off to practice what they learned during the session. This pattern is clear from the first

Citizenship School teacher Bernice Robinson's description of a typical day:

> A typical class would begin with devotions. Someone would be assigned to carry on devotions for each class night. This relaxed and warmed up the group. Then homework was checked. Then we would have about thirty minutes of reading. I wrote down each word they had difficulty in pronouncing and used these words during our spelling period, which followed. The definitions of these words were also taught so the students would understand what they were reading. Then we would have a session in arithmetic, using the prices from grocery lists, catalogue orders, etc. Then we would go thru the process of applying for a registration certificate. After which I made assignments for homework. Some nights, to maintain interest and break up the monotony of lessons, I would show a film. Highlander [Folk School] provided us with many films. Guy Carawan, who headed up the music department at Highlander, would come down and would teach singing at the classes and here again we used the words of the songs for reading. The goal of the classes was to create an awareness of the political structure in the local community, across the state, as well as nation [that] controlled funds for education, housing, employment etc. Blacks could not only be knowledgeable as to whom they should contact to eliminate what problems, but they could become candidates for these offices as well.[5]

Relying on weaving together both sacred and secular practices, Robinson opened up a space for a literacy activism that encouraged active literacy. Describing how and why she included worship tools in literacy activism, she explains, "That's where blacks used to release all of their problems[,] was through their music. They would go into those Praise Houses and shout and talk about their problems through the music. Sort of get it all out of their systems."[6]

GOOD NEWS: SACRED MUSIC AS LITERACY ACTIVISM
Black musical expressions resonated within Citizenship School activities and fostered an orientation toward a material and cultural consciousness. Gospel songs contained a mixture of Christian music based on American folk music, marked by strong rhythms and elaborate refrains while incorporating elements of spirituals, blues, and jazz. Gospel ideologies highlight black music's refusal to simplify reality or devalue emotion. Songs of faith rallied the hopes of people suffering devastating social conditions. By their very nature, gospel expressions included patterns of telling stories that echoed participants' ways of talking about literacy activism, a multirhythmic way of being that exposed cultural, spiritual, and material ways of knowing, thinking, and existing. Gospel consciousness is especially visible within the literacy activities of the Civil Rights Movement, during which participants interchanged literacy activism, spiritual knowledge, and ideas about social change and were able to do so because the processes took place in private, protected worship spaces—as did the Citizenship Schools, which met in churches, social clubs, and private prayer meetings. As Robinson illustrates, even within gatherings dedicated to learning there was an exchange between spiritual and sociopolitical ideologies. Consequently, the literacy activities of the freedom movement and gospel consciousness evolved along with the surrounding culture, as people developed innovative styles and tested inventive language in response to new expressions of traditional problems. I call this "gospel literacy."

Gospel literacy, like gospel music, contains four ruling concepts: acknowledging the burden, call-and-response, bearing witness, and finding redemption. Acknowledging the burden engages an African American intellectual tradition of embracing knowledge as power, which begins by recognizing the consequences of oppressive ideologies and epistemologies while consciously choosing a redemptive response to that oppression. Specifically, in the gospel tradition, people are empowered through a formidable understanding of local history. Although the Sea Islands were politically calm before the 1950s, they are part of a region that has a tradition, since the colonial period, of strong engagement in the struggle for African American liberation. Acknowledging the burden as a theoretical concept lends itself to an analysis that pays particular attention to the legacies and traditions of African American literacy action. In addition, it's an ideology that illuminates how the Sea Islands' Citizenship Schools project was not an isolated phenomenon but the result of an African American tradition of critical intellectual activity—an empowering response; an acknowledgement of burdens. Sea Islands Citizenship School participants invoked and deepened a tradition of intellectual control.

The second driving principle of gospel literacy is call-and-response. I depart from the common understanding of call-and-response as a spontaneous exchange that operates in almost every space in black culture. Within the ideology of gospel literacy, participants use call-and-response as an avenue to practice well-thought-out responses that change the direction of dominant social forces in and out of the community. A response that merely affirms or changes the direction of a call suggests a nonabrasive action; in gospel literacy, the response doesn't refuse to go along with the call but becomes a means of doing intellectual work to execute a strategic plan, taking authority over literacy activism.

Bearing witness, the third element of gospel literacy, treats "witnessing" as a critical intellectual practice. Witnessing—interchangeable with testifying—is a sophisticated literacy activity that consists of symbolic illustrations and recitations of an experience (individual or shared). As a literacy template, it's used to recover an epistemology that complicates the way we understand the relationship between social activism and literacy acquisition and use.

The final defining concept of gospel literacy is finding redemption. This is a theoretical model that demonstrates how the deep cultural resources that develop in African American spiritual life come into secular contexts as intellectual and spiritual literacy strategies, which enhance literacy activism. Specifically, finding redemption shifts from the standard religious doctrine of eternal salvation toward a socially literate activist principle of attaining justice in this life.

Up to this point, perspectives on African American gospel ideology engage primarily in observations limited to black sacred performances. As a religious concept, gospel music is a synthesis of West African and African American music, dance, poetry, oratory, and drama. Within African American culture, gospel expressions most often call to mind joy, hope, and expectation, including narratives that provide a sense of security. However, I treat gospel from a literacy perspective that complicates conventional understandings, a perspective that situates both community-based literacy activism and gospel as ways of being, knowing, and living. This gospel literacy perspective is based on accounts by the participants of Citizenship Schools as well as my explorations into their literacy practices, exposing a gospel consciousness that weaves together spiritual and secular concepts within literacy practices, meanings, and values. These literacy practices intersect with elements of a gospel ideology, including a narrative model derived from African epistemologies.

The gospel literacy framework is not simply an attempt to impose an alternate template onto a traditional format or to claim yet another neologism for literacy. *Freedom Writing*'s uniqueness and significance lies primarily in the way I reconceptualize the meaning of *gospel*. Understanding composition studies' rhetorical roots affords me the opportunity to draw on the word *gospel*'s Greek origins, where *evangelion* meant "good story" or "good news" (specifically, "good + spel" = good news). The current definition emerged as Old English translators went about the task of converting the Bible from Latin to English. They changed the Latin term *bona annutiatio* or *bonus numtius* into *gospel*, meaning "God's story." However, I use the term *gospel* as defined in its original incarnation of "good story" or "good news." Following a nonconformist definition provides a means of exploring Citizenship School participants' "gospel" through a narrative lens, which includes patterns of telling stories that echo the recovering thoughts about literacy. The Citizenship School participants thus used a narrative inquiry.

Freedom Writing, then, considers the literacy narratives of community-based Citizenship School participants: Bernice Robinson, Esau Jenkins, Anderson Mack, Ethel Grimball, Aileen Brewer, and finally, Guy Carawan. Robinson, a beautician and the school's first teacher, developed the original Citizenship School curriculum, teaching philosophy and classroom structure. Robinson went on to directly and indirectly train all subsequent Citizenship School teachers—if she didn't train the teachers, she trained someone who trained them. Esau Jenkins, the most prominent black community leader on Johns Island, initiated the idea for the schools and, with Robinson's help, did most of the initial organizing on the island. Anderson Mack, one of the youngest participants, became an active community organizer, responsible for getting a community and day care center established on Johns Island.[7] Ethel Grimball, a social worker, and Aileen Brewer, a former teacher, first took on the task of teaching Alice Wine to read and write. Both Grimball and Brewer went on to set up and teach schools on Wadmalaw and Edisto Islands. Finally, I explore the experiences of Guy Carawan, folk artist and musical director of the Highlander Folk School, who introduced "Eyes on the Prize" to the wider movement after Alice Wine taught him her rendition of the song.

"NOBODY KNOWS THE TROUBLE I'VE SEEN": SITUATING LITERACY

Before I move any deeper into situating gospel literacy within the story of the Citizenship Schools, I need to illuminate the landscape for defining literacy in general and African American literacy in particular.[8] Literacy here does not mean solely decoding or encoding sounds and letters, nor is it a synonym for *education*. As I interviewed participants and gathered text for this book, I recovered a wealth of primary narratives, including perspectives on how Citizenship School participants defined literacy for themselves. My literacy analysis, then, is not of the Citizenship Schools but rather of the actual participants and what they say about what literacy does within the context of African American social protest. Through my recovery, participants share how literacy acquisition became more than rote alphanumeric skills acquired for civic participation; it was a marriage between critical thinking, one's sense of self-worth, and the ability to effectively utilize socioeconomic, intellectual, and human resources. My interest in this relationship became even more intense when I learned that Alice Wine's literacy activism ranged beyond voter registration. For her it meant being able to read novels and write letters to her family in New York. Wine's experience speaks to a central shift in literacy studies, which in recent years has moved from the concept of literacy as a set of stand-alone skills to the idea of literacy as a social practice. New Literacy scholars like Brian Street explain that this shift requires acknowledging that although literacy activities are specific to individual behavior, they are shaped through social relationships and "embedded in socially constructed epistemological principles. It is about knowledge [and wisdom]: The ways in which people address reading and writing are themselves rooted in conceptions of knowledge, identity, being" (418). Thus, the socially constructed nature of literacy is evident even when an individual fills out a voter registration form. But foremost, cultural and social traditions intensify the ways in which relations within discursive communities determine both how reading and writing happen and who is able to participate.

Both participating in and researching a literacy event as extreme as the Civil Rights Movement require more than simply being able to read and write; these activities rely on adhering to the West African philosophy of *mate masie* (wisdom, knowledge, and prudence). This philosophy weaves together both wisdom and knowledge while having the good sense to consider other perspectives. Without crucial knowledge of how social customs and power dynamics within African American culture vary from one situation to the next, it is difficult to negotiate rhetorical situations and to participate in a way that is meaningful and even comprehensible to the collective (both inside and outside composition studies).

It is with an eye toward critical literacies that I treat literacy not only as the process of learning to read and write—decoding and making meaning—but also as the way these skills are linked to social contexts: in this case, the lived experience of less visible and often marginalized community-based activists. Literacy here works within the complexities of a social constructivist paradigm—it represents social status as well as identity ideology. This means that the unit of analysis is the individual *and* the community. I recognize participants as socialized members of an interpretive community. As I see it, the key to this perspective is the existence of a consensus among interlocutors. Literate activities are located within the norms of an interpretative community. Therefore, the direction of my analysis is reciprocal—from the group to the individual and the individual to the group (i.e., the learner to the teacher, the teacher to the learner, and each to a goal beyond the general description of civic inclusion).

I primarily map my literacy perspective around the ideas about literacy of Jacqueline Jones Royster and Deborah Brandt. Royster identifies literacy as a sociocognitive acquisition. She says that literacy "is the ability to gain access to information and to use this information variously to articulate lives and experiences and also to identify, think through, refine and solve problems, sometimes complex problems, over time" (*Traces* 45). Brandt illuminates how individual acts of writing are connected to larger cultural, historical, social, and political systems (*Literacy*). I find that theorizing literacy within a turbulent era of civil unrest underscores the idea of literacy's symbiotic relationship with specific contexts. It advocates for an ideological model, viewing literacy as consequential.[9] Similarly, Royster's and Brandt's definitions initiate a paradigm shift in composition studies through a methodology of recovering, while accounting for, the intersections of a material and cultural framework of literacy activity. These theories' components of literacy as a social process, including multiples stages of participation, intertextual relations, and cultural knowledge, are ways to understand not only the social process of literacy but also its multirhythmic nature as it functions in African American literacy activism.[10] I follow this body of work through my analysis of a specific grassroots literacy campaign, demonstrating how learning to teach writing and learning to write operate in this context.

In my attempt to recover these literacy narratives, I faced two obstacles familiar to most literacy historians, primarily due to literacy's individual and social implications. First, for both historical and contemporary literacy research, the primary problem is to define *literacy*. The second problem is how to clearly mark the significance of the symbiotic relationship between literacy and an event. Carl Kaestle describes the problem of defining *literacy* by explaining that "'the term literacy appears straightforward, but because it can refer to a wide range of reading and writing activities, historians' definitions vary'" (qtd. in Royster, *Traces* 3). He goes on to say that "even if restricted only to reading, the term literacy may imply a wide range of abilities." For example, the work of literacy historians such as James Anderson, Harvey Graff, Shirley Brice Heath, and Brian Street includes accounts of how literacy access—freedom and opportunity to obtain literacy and favorable circumstances to use and expand basic skills—is restricted by race, ethnicity, class, gender, religion, language, and geography.[11] These perspectives encourage me to dismantle philosophies of universal access for all groups and individuals through a rigid examination of the barriers to access experienced by members of marginalized communities. Sociolinguist James Paul Gee argues that definitions of literacy too often appeal to notions of naturalness, innocence, and individual responsibility. He maintains that this narrow perspective "obscures the multiple ways in which reading, writing and language interrelate with the workings of power and desire in social life" (27). Revisionist perspectives, however, bring attention to the ways in which access is experienced differently within racial, class, gendered, historical, social, religious, and geographical contexts.[12]

I align myself with social historians who identify the complicated layers of literacy acquisition and, more recently, attempt to examine the ideological and functional relationships between literacy and broader political ideals. Social historians include but are not limited to Janet Duitsman Cornelius, Adam Banks, Keith Gilyard ("African," "Introduction"), Deborah Brandt (*Literacy*, "Sponsors"), Catherine Prendergast, and John Duffy—scholars who, to varying degrees, place the study of literacy within larger social contexts, illuminating the material and cultural conditions that facilitate an increase in mass literacy acquisition and use.[13] Ultimately, some social historians remind us that the problems of defining literacy, historically or contemporarily, cannot be resolved by treating literacy as a stagnant, linear process. Literacies like those discussed in this book include fluctuations, strands, transactions, and divisions. The challenge becomes more complicated when combining ethnographic and historical literacy explorations.

My dilemma of how to situate myself within these perspectives intensified when I waded through the sea of archives while also interviewing participants. I searched for academic language or theories to help explain what I saw happening. Soon I discovered that the majority of existing research falls short of including language and ideologies composed from an African American perspective. Other studies of the Citizenship Schools consisted of either biographies or social historical studies, primarily within the disciplines of education and history. Listening and reading closely with respect and honor, I became increasingly frustrated in my attempt to find a methodological and theoretical perspective that includes conversations with participants, one that pays attention to literacy acquisition and use yet also speaks to an African American worldview. The problem was compounded by the fact that the vocabulary describing everyday grassroots critical intellectual activities was produced by and accessible to the educated elite, thus continuing the marginalization of the very community that actually put in the work. Consequently, I cannot abandon my position as a composition scholar. This is a difficult space to occupy. Fortunately, I can draw courage from the mandate to secure a place for black women's intellectual strategies set forth by black feminist scholars such as Patricia Hill Collins and Barbara Smith, who lead me to Royster, whose work on the rhetorical and literate history of African American women eases the strain of researching African American intellectual activities. Highlighting my task as an obligation, she challenges the scholarly community to "enrich our definition of *tradition, literacy* and *intellectualism* and . . . use this enriched vision to look *again* at the historical evidence of the ways in which black women have used their literacy" ("Perspectives" 103). Both Royster and Collins explain why my responsibility is to build an inclusive intellectual perspective, and each is worth quoting at length. Collins notes the following:

One key role for Black women intellectuals is to ask the right questions and investigate all dimensions of a Black woman's standpoint with and for African-American women. Black women intellectuals thus stand in a special relationship to the community of African-American women for which we are a part, and this special relationship frames the contours of Black feminist thought. . . . While Black feminist thought may originate with Black feminist intellectuals it cannot flourish isolated from the experiences and ideas of other groups. The dilemma is that Black women intellectuals must place our own experiences and consciousness at the center of any serious efforts to develop Black feminist thought yet not have that thought become separatist and exclusionary. (6)

The ideology that permeates Royster's and Collins's work requires us to find ways to transcend standard "composition" frameworks developed outside African American ways of knowing. Like Carmen Kynard, I accept that my orientation is "high academe" as well as "inner-personal and outer-historical" (13). These intersections are the development of enhanced intellectualism. Ultimately, I ignite my courage as a new scholar required to create innovative theoretical models that look to the culture—my culture—for identification. Royster explains this as a bold task of generating proactive models:

In forging ahead in uncharted territory, I have also had to confront directly, in the rendering of text, my own status as a researcher who identifies unapologetically with the subjects of my inquiries. In terms of my own invented ethos, within contexts that would position me otherwise because of the "marginality" of what I do, I have had to create proactive spaces rather than reactive spaces from which to speak and interpret. The task of creating new space, rather than occupying existing space, has encouraged in me the shaping of a scholarly ethos that holds both sound scholarly practices and ethical behavior in balance and harmony and that consistently projects this balancing in research and in writing. (*Traces* 252)

This call for varied methodologies originating in an African-derived cultural epistemology, where self is understood as a process of continual interaction, rests securely in a call-and-response ideology within a community, which in turn is constantly negotiating within a resistant context. As a theoretical concept, this practice is also understood as decentering. However, when this ideology is applied to African American culture, the deconstructive interrogation of self is usually predicated on the unexamined assumption that the self is constructed in Euro-American terms, which means the ideology itself needs deconstructing. Ultimately, Royster's declaration gives me permission to embrace my position as both a composition researcher and an African American woman. As a researcher, I am not *invisible*. This book unapologetically includes my perspective as the granddaughter of a Milwaukee-based Freedom School trustee and my cultural connection to an African American community. In addition, my experiences growing up in a black church taught me that I'm obligated to remain grounded in the African American sense of self, drawing strength and energy from a community capable of validating my experience.

True to her location within composition studies, Royster offers a model for the responsibility of literacy historians to push explorations into a larger context, encouraging change for individuals and the world. The task of defining literacy is to construct a theoretical framework for African American people that recognizes the autonomous and subjective value of literacy as a means of "generating action" (*Traces* 42). In my own work, I follow the outline in which she defines the multiple tasks involved in shaping this type of theoretical framework, which are:

(1) to analyze and interpret the ways in which written language and action systematically converge; (2) to document the rhetorical habits and choices of individual writers, an effort that requires attention to ethos and context, as well as to message and medium; (3) to examine patterns emerging over time, not simply to suggest, for example, that African American women seem to have an affinity for essay writing but to theorize about what such rhetorical preferences indi-

cate about connections between this group, a worldview, and their deliberate uses of written language to meet sociopolitical purposes. (43)

Royster equips historical revisionists with a means of defining the literacies of an individual, a culture, and a community. In the end, I'm a critically conscientious historian, embracing my own cultural identity while wading through the waters of Sea Islands literacy stories. Through both my ethnographic and historical research, I recover an emerging theme grounded in African American gospel concepts, which weave spiritual and secular principles into the motives, means, and methods of literacy learning and literacy activism.

CHAPTER BREAKDOWN

First and foremost, *Freedom Writing* recovers gospel literacy as a way of knowing; it is a cultural practice within an African American literacy event. In this introduction, I explain how to take on the burdens of academic conventions to develop a text that revises the intersections between an African American gospel consciousness and literacy. Chapter 1, "Like a Bridge over Troubled Water: An African American Sacred–Secular Continuum," introduces and defines gospel literacy concepts within mainstream literacy scholarship (including various disciplines) while discussing how, within these perspectives, African American women have an intellectual tradition, albeit marginalized, of consciously choosing a response to their burdens that embraces the authority to expand their own knowledge. I accomplish this through an extensive analysis of social, historical, and theoretical perspectives within composition, African American, historical, education, and women's studies. I take on studies that examine various ideologies in literacy as well as the rich diversity of African American culture. Chapter 2, "'Gonna Lay Down My Burdens': Jim Crow to Composition Studies—A Diagrammatic Perspective," draws on the gospel concept of "acknowledging the burden" to map the Citizenship School story. This chapter employs an African American tradition of embracing knowledge as power within existing perspectives. Chapter 3, "'I Got Some Pride': Call-and-Response as an Intellectual Principle of

Literacy Acquisition and Use," looks at how Sea Islands Citizenship School activities invoked "call-and-response, a culturally informed approach to literacy action that permeates notions of literacy and language. I describe how some of the fundamental dimensions of this communication pattern played out in the Civil Rights literacy crusade. Most important, I discuss how participants forged resistance against a narrow literacy learning centered on civic inclusion by drawing on gospel literacy. This chapter also demonstrates how Citizenship School participants' communal performances and emerging meanings were central to literacy acquisition and use. Chapter 4, "'I've Got a Testimony': Bearing Witness to a Historical Case of African American Curriculum and Instructional Methods," treats the gospel literacy concept of "witnessing" as an intellectual process in order to analyze the Citizenship Schools' curriculum and instructional methods. I explain how such an analysis complicates the way we understand the relationship between social activism and literacy acquisition and use. Drawing on personal interviews and actual classroom discussions, as well as lesson plans and teacher training sessions, I provide an extended analysis of the classroom-in-action, illustrating how everything is working together—witnessing, spirituality, music, curriculum, teachers, and learners. Finally, Chapter 5, "'And Still I Rise': Finding Redemption through Unceasing Variations of Literacy Acquisition and Use," situates the gospel literacy concept of "finding redemption," which embodies principles of recovery through the intersections of literacy acquisition and emancipatory power and authority, as a theoretical model for explaining the implications of gospel literacy, as well as a means to restore to a place of honor the idea that African American cultural traditions contain more than basic exercises in thought and expression.

Before I begin the following discussion, however, I need to be clear that I am taking aspects of a unified experience out of context, making it difficult to discuss one characteristic without seeing evidence of another.

1

Like a Bridge over Troubled Water: An African American Sacred–Secular Continuum

IN 1932, THOMAS DORSEY COINED THE TERM *gospel* as a music genre. Early gospel hymns reflected themes concerned with social issues of the time—racial upheavals, dislocation, nationwide poverty, the Great Depression, and mass migration. This was a time when black people in large numbers moved from rural sharecropping plantations to northern cities, primarily to find work and escape overt Jim Crow practices. Gospel music appealed because of a combination of secular rhythms and sacred/spiritual lyrics. Intricate rhythms, strong beats, and alternating scales interact simultaneously, giving equal attention to blessings and sorrows. As a result, this musical expression moved beyond the Negro spirituals, which were primarily in a European musical style pushed onto African American people. Spirituals rested on a fantasy of *hoping* for a better life in the hereafter, but gospel held tight to the *promise* of a better life right now. Thus, the gospel sound infuses black cultural consciousness and transforms it into a way of knowing.

Although the gospel tradition began its steady assent to widespread respectability during the later 1920s to early 1930s, gospel experience dates as far back as 1790, when limited worship spaces for African Americans in many cases also provided the first formal learning environments, especially for those in captivity.[1] While Dorsey is considered the most visible predecessor to combine secular blues and jazz rhythms with sacred lyrics, Charles Tindley, an African American Methodist minister born in Maryland in 1859, was the first.[2] Tindley gained prominence as a camp meeting preacher and singer and wrote lyrics to the popular Civil Rights anthem "We Shall Overcome." Tindley's lyrics were "I'll overcome, I'll overcome, I'll overcome someday." Dorsey, a converted blues and jazz musician also known as "Georgia Tom," performed with blues artist Ma Rainey and her Wild Cats Jazz Band. Dorsey was a prolific poet and songwriter and is still considered the "Father of Gospel Music." He wrote more than 400 songs, the most popular being "Bridge over Troubled Water" and "Precious Lord" (Fallin 105). The latter was sung by gospel legend Mahalia Jackson at the 1963 March on Washington and, at his request, at President Roosevelt's funeral. Dorsey's influence was not limited to African American music, as white musicians also followed his lead. "Precious Lord" has been recorded by Elvis Presley, Jim Reeves, Roy Rogers, Johnny Cash, and Tennessee Ernie Ford, among hundreds of others. It was a favorite gospel song of the Rev. Martin Luther King, Jr. and was sung at the rally in Memphis the night before his assassination. At its inception, however, members of Mainline Baptist Church in Birmingham Alabama, as well as other church leaders in the community, discouraged the use of gospel music in their churches, seeing it as too worldly and emotional.

As a form of covert political protest with double meanings, gospel discourse worked well alongside apolitical Holiness churches and, obviously, within the Civil Rights Movement. Civil Rights activist and Freedom School attendant Fannie Lou Hamer's rendition of "This Little Light of Mine" draws attention to gospel's binary. When Hamer belted out "This little light of mine, I'm gonna let it shine," she married radical secular activism with a traditionally sacred song, announcing that her activism would illuminate the world when she sat at the front of the bus and placed a ballot in the voting box. Hamer's "light" translates into full participation in American society.

Ultimately, the gospel sound has its roots firmly planted in southern cotton fields. Gospel anthems clearly merge work songs, spirituals, and the rhythms of juke joints. I am not the first to see the intersection of sacred and secular ideologies in gospel music. Both history and composition scholars have considered the role of gospel expressions beyond religious boundaries. While most people consider the church as the space for sacred activities and secular territory the space for everything else, historian Lawrence Levine combines the two in a short but important section of his text *Black Culture and Black Consciousness.* His perspective supplies a rationale for gospel expression as a way of knowing that is linked to cultural consciousness. He recognizes the often contradictory intersections between black cultural dynamics and black intellectual consciousness, acknowledging that black cultural consciousness provides the means for black people to act on their own behalf and respond to oppression in the ways they choose. I would argue that Levine builds a framework for developing gospel expression, carefully connecting the writings of poet-author Langston Hughes, blues singer T-Bone Walker, Jazz bassist Pops Foster, and folklorist Zora Neal Hurston, affirming pre-Dorsey secular influences. I would argue that Levine's research points to Hughes and Foster for bringing attention to false boundaries between black sacred and secular consciousness. He quotes Langston Hughes during a visit to a Holiness worship service in Chicago: "'I was entranced by their stepped-up rhythms, tambourines, hand clapping and uninhibited dynamics, rivaled only by Ma Rainey [Dorsey's blues club partner] singing the blues at the old Monogram Theater. . . . The music of these less formal Negro churches took hold of me, moved me and thrilled me'" (qtd. in Levine 180). Hughes's observation parallels blues singer T-Bone Walker's affirmation of complex sacred–secular ideologies. Walker explains that "'the first time I ever heard a boogie-woogie [a kind of jazz] piano was the first time I went to church'" (qtd. in Levine 180). Walker's experience with religious and worldly intersections occurred at a Dallas Holy Ghost church where a preacher used a "bluesy tone" to excite the congregation. Beyond Dorsey there are many examples of sacred conversions to secular expressions and vice versa, also known as "crossing-over." Historical examples include the songs of Sam Cooke, Otis Redding, Stevie Wonder, and Ray Charles, who explains that

> gospel and the blues are really, if you breaks it down, almost the same thing. It's just a question of whether you're talkin' about a woman or God. I come out of the Baptists church

and naturally whatever happened to me in the church is gonna spill over. So I think the blues and gospel music is quite synonymous to each other. (Charles qtd. in Werner, *Change* 31) [3]

Gospel, like the blues, centers on making human suffering bearable. Holding its fixed position within human frailty, gospel consciousness motivates a vision of promise. This principle also operates in the music of contemporary artists such as Whitney Houston, Aretha Franklin, and Patti LaBelle. Each consistently practices a fluid back-and-forth movement between sacred and secular expression.

The intellectual and cultural intersection between African and African American sacred and secular ways of knowing is not an entirely new concept. This perspective is inherent in African-derived epistemologies that transition into African American intellectual scholarship dating back to the pedagogical visions of Carter G. Woodson, Anna Julia Cooper, and W. E. B. DuBois. Joseph E. Holloway argues that even before the nightmare of captivity, Africans held strong protective attitudes toward their communities, the core of which operated at the intersection of economic, political, and religious learning. For example, Angela Davis's and Deborah Gray White's Afrafeminist work on enslaved African women confirms that the roles within African communities were clearly defined, with women fulfilling essential functions as keepers of the ancestral heritage. In addition, social historians have explained that although enslaved Africans originated from various African societies, they created common understandings with distinct institutions, religious beliefs, and kinship roles during the Middle Passage and beyond.

In composition studies, Shirley Wilson Logan (*"We Are Coming"*), Keith Gilyard ("African American"), and Geneva Smitherman (*Talkin' and Testifyin'*) jump-started research on African-derived patterns of response and action, identifying thematic structures basic to African American liberators' discourse. Each offers a theoretical model demonstrating the complex intersections between African and African American sacred communication patterns and temporal ideologies. Enslaved Africans mastered West African–derived patterns of response and action. Logan, for instance, describes how African American women's discourse shares persuasive principles with their West African ancestral communication roots. Through a recovery of Maria Stewart's rhetorical practices, Logan makes a case for black women who "evoked Africa's spirit" in their persuasive discourse (*"We Are Coming"* 24). This reminds us that the value of careful reconstructions includes the ideologies of group identity. Most important here is the inclusion of West African interactional patterns within African American discourse. Some scholars, like Elaine Richardson, have traced the spiritual vision of African American culture from Africa through the Caribbean to American classrooms and finally to street corners and hip-hop clubs. Similarly, Robinson's account demonstrates how the classroom practices of Citizenship Schools include evidence of the ways in which African American people incorporate religious ideologies into their methods of narration as well as their acquisition of knowledge. These methods of narration, like literacy stories, include a constant interchange between secular and religious responsibility.

For most scholars of composition/rhetoric, the connection between sacred and secular ideologies is familiar from Geneva Smitherman's *Talkin' and Testifyin'.* She describes this practice through a linguistic lens, showing how, within black culture, the line between sacred and secular ways of knowing is blurred. Smitherman confirms this assertion, claiming that "each discourse mode is manifested in Black American culture on a sacred-secular continuum" (103). More often than not within African life, "there are no 'irreligious people' and to be without religion amounts to a self-excommunication from the entire life of society. . . . African people do not know how to exist without religion" (91). Religion, then, is not an optional practice; it's a necessary one. Most important here is the view that religious observations are in line with the African concept of *Ubuntu,* which means "I am because we are." This philosophy rests on the belief that individual existence (and knowledge) is contingent on relationships with others. Sacred and secular ways of knowing cannot—within an African worldview—exist separately.

Without question, in African American communities the church is traditionally the most influential and long-standing institution, wielding significant political power (indicated by the number of politicians parading through Sunday worship service during election season). Consider the 2008 presidential campaign and the concern with Barack Obama's church membership. A campaign highlight was Obama's relationship with Reverend Jeremiah Wright—who, like Martin Luther King Jr., preached a radical form of black Christian autonomy. If Obama hadn't renounced Wright, his entire campaign might have been derailed. Political affiliations are often examined alongside sacred ideologies. A popular Civil Rights example is the Martin/Malcolm dichotomy. In the black community, Martin Luther King Jr.'s Christian beliefs proved more acceptable than Malcolm X's Islamic activism. Gospel tradition marries political, social, and spiritual consciousness into a way of knowing, even though gospel as a musical expression is practiced primarily in African American religious contexts. To the extent that any political agenda embraces a broad spectrum of African American communities, it must be grounded in the institutions and forms of expression that connect community with individual consciousness.

Because of its dual and subversive uses, gospel music became a logical choice for the protest anthems of the Civil Rights Movement, which drew its leaders, its vision, and much of its organization from black churches. Soon the "gospel sound," like the movement itself, began generating attention outside the South. And history shows that southern states ignited national attention to the Civil Rights Movement, giving birth to a handful of literacy initiatives that linked the individual acquisition of learning to a fundamental transformation of self and society. The black church sheltered literacy activism, which included performance and music. Some participants, like Bernice Reagon (*Voices*), linked literacy to music, maintaining that literacy, like music, was the soul of the Civil Rights Movement. If we understand literacy from this perspective, we can clearly see the relationship between literacy activism and the

Civil Rights Movement. Both illuminate visions—ways of knowing —that include a continual interchange between secular and sacred ideologies. Like the literacy activities of the freedom movement, the gospel consciousness evolved along with the surrounding culture, constantly asserting the ultimate moral connection of political and cultural experiences capable of empowering both the individual and the community. This awareness is intensely situated in an African American tradition of resisting Euro-American institutions that perpetuate the oppression of black people, including the denial of full citizenship rights. A gospel way of knowing insists on a complex intellectual understanding of the ever-changing demands of the moment as a precondition for social and political activism.

A gospel consciousness evolves when a parallel is drawn between African American literacy activism and elements of gospel ideologies. It's important to note that gospel expression and African American gospel concepts have been adopted and adapted by many cultures; however, the focus of this study is on gospel in African American communities as a way of being, acting, knowing, and living: gospel literacy. This knowledge, shared within the community, formed a relationship with literacy acquisition and use to become an integral part of the Citizenship School curriculum. When Robinson explains how she combined gospel music with the reading curriculum, she describes the role of the Highlander Folk School's musical director: "Guy Carawan, who headed up the music department at Highlander would come down and would teach singing at the classes and here again we used the words of the songs for reading [exercises]."[4] Robinson's teaching practices raise questions about how a gospel consciousness operates within literacy practices. Specifically, how does literacy—reading and writing—function within a gospel ethos? And how do African American ways of knowing, which appear to be primarily performance or cultural expressions, move beyond individual activities toward literacy acquisition and use? Exploring this inquiry exposes how, within African American culture, gospel is conceptual: it is located within a constellation of African American intellectual activism.

GOSPEL LITERACY: A WORKING DEFINITION

In this chapter, I lay out the four core concepts of gospel literacy before moving into the Citizenship School literacy narrative, offering a revised perspective on this grassroots effort. I want readers to hear the voices of Citizenship School participants, but at the same time I want to make the gospel literacy framework accessible. At the risk of oversimplifying the rich complexity of African American literacies, I organize *Freedom Writing* around the fundamental components of gospel consciousness: call-and-response, acknowledging the burden, bearing witness, and finding redemption. I apply these principles on multiple levels: in the organization of the book, in the examination of the narratives, and in the analysis of the practices, meanings, and values of literacy.

Call-and-Response

During the nightmare of captivity, enslaved Africans were forbidden to meet in large groups except when gathering for religious observations. It was here that call-and-response became a fundamental means of unifying enslaved Africans. To the outsider, it appeared to be exclusively an artistic performance, but in reality call-and-response became a unifying experience requiring active involvement between participants.

Call-and-response is probably one of the most identifiable African-derived discourse patterns. Definitions of *call-and-response* generally describe it as an expression of both ritualized communal unity and a spontaneous expression of individual freedom (see also Werner, *Playing*; and Moss, *Community* 89). As a ritual, call-and-response has been traced to African communication systems such as drumming, in which messages are delivered from village to village.[5] It has also been linked to other African communication strategies that authenticate unity, such as the relationship between a dancer and a drummer when a dancer responds to the drummer's call. Call-and-response transcends common Western norms that separate actor and audience. It is participatory in nature, not meant to be watched or observed. For example, during the era of enslavement, call-and-response was a communication strategy used to guide participants along the Underground Railroad. Collaborators most often used music to call out coded messages that could be understood and appropriately responded to only by people in harmony with the abolitionist cause. Like the communication systems between African villages, call-and-response was used by enslaved Africans as a means of communication between plantations. This tactic eventually became a central characteristic of African American music (Smitherman, *Talkin' and Testifyin'* 104–8).

As gospel literacy practice, call-and-response is the relationship between individual autonomy and critical analysis. Craig Werner eloquently describes this relationship:

> Call and response begins with the call of a leader who expresses his/her own voice through the vehicle of a traditional song, story, or image. This call, which provides a communal context for exploration of the "individual" emotion, itself responds to a shared history that suffuses later stages of the process. If the community, as it exists in the ever-changing present, recognizes and shares the experience evoked by the call, it responds with another phrase, again usually traditional, which may either affirm or present a different perspective on the initial call. Whether it affirms or critiques the initial call, however, the response enables the leader to go on exploring the implications of the material. Rich in political implications, this cultural form enables both individual and community to define themselves, to validate their experiences in opposition to dominant social forces. When working most effectively, this process requires individuals not to seek a synthesis, to deny the extreme aspects of their own experiences, but to assert their subjectivity in response to other, equally personal and equally extreme, assertions of experience. Call-and-Response, then, is African American analysis: a process that, by admitting diverse voices and diverse experiences, supports a more inclusive critique than any individual analysis. (*Playing* xvii)

The core of call-and-response is a West African ethos of valuing an interrelationship between individuals and community. Call-and-response is an intellectual course of action that requires careful thought—an integral element of literacy. Practitioners must engage in an individual process of decoding and making meaning for use in a larger context, all of which is bound by time and space.

Two key call-and-response characteristics are highlighted within the context of the Citizenship Schools' literacy activities: the initial call and the response. Both rely on a shared history that spreads through each stage of the teaching and learning process. This shared understanding can either affirm or create an alternate perspective on the initial call, refusing to accept dominant social forces. Call-and-response begins with an initial call from a leader. A successful call relies on an individual or individuals with first-rate organizational skills because leaders are expected to both motivate and stimulate the group toward active participation. A good leader must manifest strength, energy, and enthusiasm to make a group want to participate (Reagon, *Voices* 4–10).[6]

On receipt and recognition of the experience motivated by the initial call, a response is expressed, which will either affirm (repeat) the call or offer an alternate destination or goal. In the musical context, this characteristic of call-and-response (creating new meanings) involves transcending the Western practice of separating the performer and the audience. As a way of knowing, call-and-response makes literacy participatory in nature; it is a communal activity and not to be observed from afar. In musical terms, this practice is called "worrying the line," which means creating new meanings for each particular moment.

Though it is often viewed as mere social orchestration, call-and-response is a site of critical negotiation. The concept of changing direction is complex. In the context of the Citizenship Schools, literacy learning was fluid and rhythmic, and the participants were in harmony with a collective purpose: teaching and learning. The response makes way for developing new meanings. At the same time, call-and-response is about forging resistance to dominant ideologies. Resistance, in a gospel literacy sense, means rejecting a narrow, civic-centered focus for literacy acquisition and use. In other words, forging resistance—a key characteristic of the response—manipulates literacy acquisition and use beyond the initial call from the leader.

It is important to recognize that the initial call and the subsequent response rely on a shared history that permeates later stages of the teaching and learning process. A shared history includes a key principle that is also embedded in my definition of *literacy*: literacy takes place in social contexts bound by both time and space. I expand on Beverly Moss's principle of shared knowledge to include shared history, complicating the ways in which individual acts of composition are attached to larger social systems bound by time and space (Moss, *Community* 7–9; see also Brandt, *Literacy*). In the case of the Citizenship Schools, literacy activism was a response that followed from a collective history, proving that with increased knowledge, some relief or freedom from oppressive Jim Crow practices could be gained over time. Understanding gospel literacy as a complex social process makes room for questions about how literacy operates on a time-and-space continuum. What is left to consider is how language and learning responses, which are grounded in a shared history, are influenced by or connected to assumptions, practices, and values involved in teaching and learning.[7]

Before proceeding, it is useful to acknowledge perspectives that help to place gospel concepts in general, and call-and-response specifically, within a Civil Rights and literacy learning framework. Chappell, Reagon (*Voices*), and Werner (*Change*) all clearly show that during the Civil Rights Movement, African American people relied on singing not just as a means of motivating people to action but also to provide a sense of security for the individual and the group. This sense of security was essential during marches, sit-ins, and gatherings, especially when activists faced known and unknown dangers. Reagon's perspective on call-and-response is particularly useful for several reasons. She is a researcher of African American culture whose work is based on firsthand experience. Her social activist crusades as well as her singing roots began when she was a member of the Student Nonviolent Coordinating Committee (SNCC), a leading Civil Rights organization. In her description of African American congregational singing, Reagon points out that the "style has its own set of aesthetics and principles that govern the birthing and execution of a song, its own parameters defining the range and use of the vocal instrument, and its own rules setting out roles for *all* singers within the group. Traditionally, Black American congregational-style singing is initiated by the songleader" (*Voices* 4, emphasis mine). This is important because it confirms the need for an intellectual process, which requires careful thought as well as emotional engagement. Reagon emphasizes that call-and-response is not a random style of discourse or exchange; this style of communication requires specific "principles that govern" the exchange:

> The Black American traditional chorus is essential to the making of a song. The call of the song leader requires the response of the group; the raising of a new line needs the group for completion. Black American group singing builds gradually, each singer creating a musical path for each performance. The song may be known by all, but with each singing there is the potential for a new line, a different variant on the melody, new slides, and improvised calls; the traditional chorus feels its way harmonically into the chord, with patterns becoming strongest at the cadences. The song does not begin in neat, four-part-harmony; the melody is always strongest. It may be sung by all voices in unison, or some voices may sing the first or even the second octave above or below. Deviations occur, however, as each singer strives to state the melody individually. (*Voices* 6–7)

Smitherman's long-standing description of call-and-response is still widely used in composition, feminist, and African American studies. She defines *call-and-response* as follows: "[the] spontaneous verbal and non-verbal interaction between speaker and listener in which all of the statements ('calls') are punctuated by expressions ('responses') from the listener" (104). For Smitherman, call-and-response is an integral mode of discourse in which the audience constantly participates by responding to the speaker. In most cases, audience members act as coproducers of the text or discourse. Smitherman differs from researchers who treat call-and-response as a strict linear utterance–answer phenomenon, equivalent to Western classical notions of "dialogue." Rather, she treats it as an oral practice that usually involves simultaneous and overlapping utterances. Like Robert Stepto, who uses call-and-response as a linear model for African American literary history in *From Behind the Veil*, Smitherman primarily treats call-and-response as an organizing principle within African American culture, arguing that it helps "black folk to achieve the unified state of balance or harmony which is fundamental to the traditional [African] world view" (*Talkin' and Testifyin'* 105). In her discussion of call-and-response, Smitherman exchanges secular and sacred for oral and written texts. For example, on music she writes:

> The music of black groups (sacred and secular) well exemplifies the call-response tradition. Characteristically, a group is composed of a lead singer ("caller") and his or her background ("responders"). The lead opens the song and sets the initial mood, but the roles may reverse so that the leader responds to the call of the others. The direction and execution of the song depend on the mutual forces of the leader in spiritual combination with his or her background. (110)

This perspective complicates call-and-response by emphasizing the cross-cultural communication challenges this practice can present, arguing that whenever African Americans communicate, call-and-response flourishes. Smitherman adds: "The dynamics of black communication allows for individual variation within the structure. Thus all responses are 'correct'; the only 'incorrect' thing you can do is not respond at all" (108).

Most pertinent to my work is Smitherman's use of call-and-response as a teaching tool. She states that "since blacks communicate best by interacting with one another, they can also learn best by interacting with one another" (*Talkin' and Testifyin'* 220). She provides examples suggesting the benefits of either pairing students or putting them in groups that allow them to move freely about the classroom as they "learn new information and practice educational skills" (220). She continues, "Just as blacks aren't passive communicators or listeners, they aren't passive learners" (220). Smitherman argues that using call-and-response as a pedagogical strategy allows more advanced students to share with less advanced students. This was indeed an intellectual activity operating in Citizenship Schools' teaching and learning methods. According to Smitherman's description, call-and-response as an instructional model has dual benefits. First, the less advanced student improves by tightening his or her grasp of the material in a "nonthreatening and familiar form of educational exchange (learning from a peer who speaks his or her lingo); the more advanced student tightens up and enhances his or her knowledge of the same subject" (220). It is important to note that Smitherman has in mind a traditionally structured 1977 classroom, quite a difference from the unconventional 1955 South Carolina Sea Islands' Citizenship School classrooms, where African American adults were taking up literacy learning. Interestingly, Smitherman cautions that this teaching strategy requires "skillful classroom management" (suggesting that instructors should have some formal training). She argues for tapping into and teaching students "cognitive competencies, intellectual processes, and ways of seeking knowledge using whatever dialect the students possess" (220).

Most composition scholars of African American literacies will recognize Beverly Moss's perspective on call-and-response. Her work is central to understanding call-and-response as a principle of social literacy, identifying three key components of literacy as a social practice that she explores in the context of African American churches. Moss explains them as "the presence of multiple participants in the literacy event; the presence of intertextual relationships; and the influence of cultural norms and ideology that shape the way participants, intertextuality, and discourse interact" (*Community* 7). The social nature of literacy complicates levels of participation because it requires that multiple participants be included in the literacy process. For example, Moss looks at the relationship between the minister and the congregation to examine the call-and-response principle of shared knowledge, arguing that in the context of the African American churches she discusses, call-and-response is used to eliminate distance between an individual (the preacher) and the group (congregation). She further argues that this is a complicated act because, like the teacher–student relationship, the move from the pew to the pulpit tends to signal a sense of distance from the congregation:

> To be effective preachers, these ministers must simultaneously create bonds between them and their congregations. In other words, they must build trust between their congregations and themselves; they must build their own identities as part of the congregation. At the same time, these ministers must show that they are leaders worthy of standing in the pulpit before the congregation. (65)

Moss goes on to explain that a key to negotiating boundaries lies in the fact that the preachers she observes

> share [with the congregation] a history, cultural backgrounds (ethnic, popular, and so on), religious beliefs, and community values, among other things. It is because of this knowledge of audience that these ministers are able to establish community ties and construct a community identity. . . . Speaking in terms of group membership is one of the most effective and obvious strategies that each minister uses to construct community identity. (*Community* 65–66)

Moss sets the stage for examining parallels between the teacher and the preacher roles in literacy learning, arguing that the African American minister's sermon is not a monologue but rather "a dialogue between the minister and congregation in which the minister directs the dialogue but the congregation participates in the dialogue by providing feedback. This call-and-response dialogue is characterized by feedback from the congregation that urges the minister on" (*Community* 64). Finally, Moss establishes that call-and-response contains components of "participatory feedback," which reaches past religious gatherings "to most aspects of public performance in African-American communities (political rallies, concerts, movies)" (89). Within the Citizenship Schools, for example, instructors like Bernice Robinson situated themselves as part of the group while simultaneously maintaining the proper amount of space from the group necessary for instruction.

While this work on call-and-response is culturally revealing, none of the scholarship has looked at call-and-response as it was actually used in a particular setting within the Civil Rights Movement. Call-and-response is traditionally examined in relation to religious, literary, or musical performance, or, more recently, within composition studies, as either a rhetorical or literate strategy (see also Smitherman, *Talkin' and Testifyin'*; Foster; Moss, *Community*). In addition, call-and-response has been treated in African American rhetorical studies as a West African–derived dialogic communication process (see also Alkebulan; Woodyard). On the other hand, literacy researchers such as Heath usually treat call-and-response as a literacy activity confined to the primary classroom.

Freedom Writing draws on, extends, and responds to previous studies by explaining, from a historical perspective, how call-and-response operated within the context of the Citizenship Schools, where it was an embedded learning and teaching strategy. Ultimately, I treat it as an intellectual activity rather than a general cultural or literacy practice (like giving sermons or performing).

When call-and-response is situated in a particular place and time, in this case the Sea Islands Citizenship Schools, we see critical intellectual work being performed by "ordinary" grassroots people, such as Esau Jenkins and Bernice Robinson. In this context, call-and-response operates out of an intellectual tradition that connects literacy practices, meanings, and values with individual and group autonomy. Through call-and-response, participants define themselves while validating their collective experiences. Most important in this context, call-and-response represents a crucial intellectual activity because it requires considerable coherent thinking and logical reasoning. In addition, it provides a means for the researcher as well as the participant(s) (group and individual) to explore literacy learning material, means, and methods, including the assertion of literacy learning autonomy.

Acknowledging the Burden

The second component of gospel literacy, "acknowledging the burden," relies on one primary conviction: that history and power are synonymous. The combination of history and power—or power in history—is essential to an understanding of acknowledging the burden. Rarely is the term *burden* associated with optimism, encouragement, motivation, or even power. The combination of history and power—or power in history—are essential here. In the gospel consciousness, however, acknowledging the burden moves beyond a history of suffering, linking individual and community experiences and weaving together individual and group practices, meanings, and values. Ultimately, a burden in the gospel tradition does not revolve around suffering, helplessness, or despair. On the contrary, it is an empowering practice motivating participants to choose a liberating response. For example, the lyrics to the song "We Shall Overcome" spell out a sense of belief that success *is* imminent. They do this not in an arrogant way but with a confident assurance that participants are standing up for what's right. At its heart, acknowledging the burden relies on spiritual principles such as freedom, hope, courage, and perseverance, which people use to consciously and aggressively resist systems of oppression. One of the criticisms leveled at nonmaterial values or ethereal pursuits is that the decision to teach writing from this perspective is trendy and without historical precedent. However, as I demonstrate in Chapter 2, it can serve politically as a positive example of the kind of reform that writing studies wants to promote. Similarly, when opponents of Afracentric sacred ideologies argue that such issues as race and gender have nothing to do with teaching or learning, the response should be that sacred and secular issues have always served as empowering material for the acquisition of knowledge.

People understand power in a number of ways. A scientist might say that it's the ability to move an object or to act. A community organizer might say that power is the strength to organize people. For a community activist during the 1950s, power was the wisdom to identify a specific phenomenon, such as the increased national interest in human rights, and acquire the knowledge to make the moment act in a desired manner. This is what it means to identify power not from the ground *up*, but from the ground *out*. Rarely do institutions of power and prestige treat a "misfortune" or "hardship" as empowering. However, unpacking acknowledging the burden as a way of knowing—a literate practice—represents moving past suffering, helplessness, or despair. Acknowledging the burden demonstrates how history changes when people take authority over their literacy practices.

Bearing Witness

Researchers in critical theory, musicology, African American studies, and composition studies have argued that testifying, or "bearing witness," is not simple commentary but rather dramatic narration requiring a communal reenactment of one's feelings and experiences (see Moss, *Community*; Reagon; Smitherman, *Talkin' and Testifyin'*; Werner, *Playing*; H. Williams). Similar to call-and-response, the group interaction reaffirms individual humanity by helping to dismiss any sense of isolation. A testimony is usually a specific story about a tragedy or bad time(s) a person has experienced and how a higher or greater power has brought that person though the difficult experience. Thus, testimonies are rhetorically sophisticated symbolic examples of an individual or shared experience. Within the black church, witnessing establishes a communal bond by narrating a detailed and specific experience.[8]

I draw my definition of *testifying* primarily from Geneva Smitherman, who in *Talkin' and Testifyin'* explains that these characteristics come out of the Black Church and are part of the African American traditions that form black semantics. Smitherman defines *testifying* as follows:

> *Testifyin,* concepts referring to a ritualized form of black communication in which the speaker gives verbal witness to the efficacy, truth and power of some experience in which all blacks have shared. In the church, testifyin is engaged in on numerous symbolic occasions; newly converted ex-"sinners" testify to the church congregation the experience of being saved, for instance, or on Watch Meeting Night, New Years Eve, when church folk gather to "watch" the old year go out and the new one come in—they testify to the goodness of the Lord during the past year. A spontaneous expression to the

church community, testifyin can be done whenever anybody feels the spirit—it don't have to be no special occasion. Like Rev. C. L. Franklin, father of Aretha Franklin, might just get up in the pulpit any Sunday morning and testify to the goodness of God. Aretha talks about the greatness of her man and how he makes her feel in her well-known blues recording, *Dr. FEELGOOD,* and that's testifyin too. (58)

Testifying or bearing witness permeated literacy acquisition and use in the Citizenship Schools and in fact could be seen to share principles with literacy learning.[9] In the gospel culture, the practice of testifying complicates a traditional narrative by including either an account of or a response to a burden or problem ("acknowledging the burden," as discussed). Interestingly, Smitherman's definition of *testifying* includes rhetorical principles such as persuasive empowerment acquired by reporting on a triumph, success, or good thing (e.g., *Dr. FEELGOOD*) in order to persuade the community or group to believe in a higher power or greater force (e.g., God). In Chapter 4, for example, Bernice Robinson gives an account that includes both her personal knowledge about literacy acquisition and use and her lived experience or testimony. She recounts her feelings about how her previous traditional educational experiences led her to fear teaching and how her previous learning experiences inform her nervousness and lack of confidence on the first night of class. However, within her testimony about that initial class, Robinson gives a stronger power (the community or God) credit for her success in gaining control over past oppressive learning experiences and her efforts not to bring that into the classroom. Similar to the gospel literacy concepts of call-and-response and acknowledging the burden, bearing witness contains specific communicative and epistemological principles and characteristics that intersect with literacy and larger social systems. In the case of the Citizenship Schools, these social systems are not limited to the larger Civil Rights Movement, but instead encompass a shared belief in a transformative spiritual power.

In bearing witness, literacy and rhetoric—both written and oral —frequently work together. Historically, African Americans have had to make "the Word" their own in order to construct language. As Janet Cornelius's work illustrates, for example, for many enslaved people the Bible provided the community with an identity. Admittedly, this acquisition of knowledge was connected to the legacy of colonial missionary literacy. Rejecting this legacy of oppression, African Americans spoke the Word through reading and writing as an act of resistance and an assertion of identity. In African American rhetorical studies, this practice has been identified as *Nommo*. According to composition scholar Keith Gilyard, *Nommo* "is the belief in the pervasive, mystical, transformative, even life-giving power of the Word" ("Introduction" 12). Smitherman adds that African Americans reinterpret this linguistic orientation as a way to actualize the "fundamental unity between the spiritual and material aspects of existence" (*Talkin' and Testifyin'* 75). She concludes that "the oral tradition, then, is part of the cultural baggage the African brought to America. Preslavery background was one in which the concept of *Nommo,* the magic power of the Word, was believed necessary to actualize life and give man mastery over things" (*Talkin' and Testifyin'* 77–78).[10] The African belief in the power and necessity of *Nommo* was so strong that a verbal battle was required to precede or accompany warfare. We see this performance being acted out in the Citizenship Schools' teaching and learning activities. For example, as I explore in more depth later in this chapter, school participants, through the acquisition of knowledge, gained power over the list of "offenses," or the words on the South Carolina voter registration form, by gaining mastery over the words—learning how to pronounce them and the actual meanings. In Bernice Robinson's recollection of a lesson based on voter registration forms, we see the principle of *Nommo* in action:

> As they would read and I taught them to read, every word they stumbled over we came to a spelling lesson and I'd pull the words out, put them on the board, break them into syllables and give the explanation, what the word means. I told Myles one night (Myles was down here in class) and I was having this lesson. I was just going down this list, giving them

the meaning of this word just from the top of my head. I was looking at the board and there were a couple of words I didn't know the meaning of, and I said, "Mmm, this word here means something." And Myles and I just laughed at that. If I hadn't realized, you know we use words that we don't know the meaning of, and rather than have them read this section of the Constitution and just call words and not know what it was, that they were being required to read. This is how we got started in our program. (Robinson, Thrasher and Wigginton Interview)

For Citizenship School participants, completing a voter registration application was more than a simple lesson in filling out an application or learning vocabulary words. A deeper lesson in the power of words was taking place.

Most crucial in my breakdown of bearing witness is the spiritual element underlying a testifying ideology. In the musical tradition, for example, a gospel singer responds by testifying or bearing witness to a problem, dilemma, or "the trouble they've seen," sharing the most sincere truths they know. But the testimony doesn't stop at acknowledging the burden; it also recognizes the presence of a power or spirit greater than the force behind the burden. In a sacred context, this is usually recognized through nonverbal expressions such as moans or shouts. Kimmika L. H. Williams argues that "the ontology of African-influenced spirituality includes (1) God (2) spirits (3) men and women, (4) plants and animals, and (5) inanimate objects or 'things'" (93). Craig Werner discusses the multiple identities and interpretations of a higher power within African American culture, stating that

it takes an energy bigger than yourself, the wellspring of healing that South African pianist Abdullah Ibrahim called "water from an ancient well." For the classic gospel singers, the source is God; for soul singers, it's love. Bob Marley calls it Jah. George Clinton envisions Atlantis, the Mothership. Arrested Development imagines a tree in Tennessee. (*Change* 30–31)

It's important to add that acknowledging this power also includes an expectation of being saved, delivered, or rescued from the oppressive force by a superior, higher, and more powerful force. No matter how the power is identified, however, personal power and autonomy includes communal liberation. Survival depends on bearing witness to a connection with a higher power.

A testimony expresses what we share individually when coincidences and miracles happen, providing evidence of a dominant energy or power—God—that could not be explained through material means. Witnessing provides personal knowledge about a time or space when individuals were confronted with evidence of a higher power they could not deny. This force is spiritual, real, and central to testimonies within gospel literacy. For example, Bernice Robinson didn't know where or how she acquired her instructional methods, declaring, "I don't know yet how I did it. It was something that hit me when talking. . . . I don't know yet how I did it" (Thrasher and Wigginton Interview)

Within African American gospel practices, witnessing has both sacred and secular implications. It is a communicative, rhetorical practice with spiritual, nonmaterial dimensions including faith, hope, courage, willingness, humility, unconditional love, perseverance, open-mindedness, awareness, vigilance, self-discipline, sharing, caring, and service. In the black church, witnessing is a way of verbally acknowledging and affirming the power of God by openly recognizing or affirming a significant experience outside the sacred context. A conventional definition of *witnessing* is "to testify by giving an account of something," reporting on or explaining a situation or event that the speaker has personal knowledge of. In sacred contexts, witnessing includes visual accounts, prophetic experiences, testimonies, or narratives. Basically, it's the retelling of a story. However, the purpose of witnessing is to persuade or communicate valuable life-giving or life-changing knowledge. Smitherman (*Talkin' and Testifyin'*) explains that in the Black Church a testimony is usually delivered in dramatic fashion, re-creating a spiritual reality for the listener, who at the moment shares, vicariously, the experience that the testifier has gone through (e.g., testifying about the oppressive activities of Jim Crow).

I define *literacy* as a way of knowing, a process by which decoding and making meaning take place in social contexts: in other words, individual acts of composition (reading and writing) are attached to larger social systems. Here I use that definition to illustrate how literacy acquisition and use intersect with witnessing—a practice of communicating valuable knowledge as well as life experiences and relating them to a larger social system, in this case the larger Civil Rights Movement. Bearing witness, then, includes the testimonies or personal knowledge and individual accounts that infuse the practices, meanings, and values of literacy, becoming central to Citizenship School participants' literacy acquisition and use.

Finding Redemption

Gospel literacy gets taken up with conscious attention to a tradition of African American epistemologies, which are determined by specific principles. I draw on Hurston because she helps to reiterate the theme that opened this text: it is important to acknowledge and understand historical events before we can make meaning from them and address contemporary concerns. Hurston states:

> Like the dead-seeming, cold rocks, I have memories within that came out of the material that went to make me. Time and Place have had their say. So you will have to know something about the time and place where I came from, in order that you may interpret the incidents and directions of my life. (561)

Through Hurston's assertion, we see that concepts of understanding and interpretation provide a place to begin considering the conscious, theoretical intellectualisms that intersect with African American cultural norms.

The gospel concept of "finding redemption" demonstrates how principles of recovery—through emancipatory power and authority—permeate the incidents and directions of composition research and teaching. The general connotations of redemption are usually located almost exclusively within a Christian ideology of individual deliverance from transgressions, which can be obtained only through the acceptance of Jesus Christ. For African American people, this deliverance is almost always rewarded after death. Historically, white Christians in the United States used the idea of redemption as a means to oppress and dominate African Americans. During the era of enslavement, for example, Eurocentric images of God and Jesus Christ were dangled in front of African captives as the ultimate master they should seek to please if they wanted to be "free." However, for African American people, God is a transformer of current consciousness. This ideology is the basis for a resource that enables people to maintain the human image without completely acquiescing to the norms of the oppressor (see also Fulop and Raboteau).

For African Americans, the concept of finding redemption shifts from the standard religious doctrine of eternal salvation toward attaining justice in this life. Charles Long, in his essay "Perspectives for a Study of African-American Religion in the United States," explains that traditionally in African American culture, God appears as an all-powerful and moral deity. However, the fundamental distinction between God and Jesus Christ is crucial, a distinction so important that when the language of Christianity is used, African Americans traditionally hold to the Trinitarian distinction, although adherence to this distinction has been for experiential rather than dogmatic reasons (62). Thus, gospel redemption breaks down the difference between an individual theory of life-here-after-salvation and a collective, experienced, right-here-right-now-liberation. In other words, as Werner states, "If we are going to bear up under the weight of the cross, find the strength to renounce the Devil, if we're going to survive to bear witness and move on, we're going to have to connect [to a higher power, to ourselves, to each other, in this life]" (*Change* 31). Finding redemption, for my purposes, is a means of explaining how deep cultural resources that develop in the church and spiritual life transfer to a secular context as intellectual and spiritual strategies that enhance literacy activism.[11]

As a theoretical model, finding redemption redeems the Citizenship School narrative. It also provides a means for me to restore—get back, recover—African American cultural traditions as a critical intellectual exercise in thought and expression. Gospel literacy, like the Civil Rights Movement, is really committed to wide-ranging social transformation. The gospel literacy approach sees personal redemption (as understood by the participants themselves) as the path to individual, communal, and global transformation. This approach has local, national, and international implications (for life on the Sea Islands, the broader Movement, and the redemption of African and US culture). My focus is on the local aspects of redemption, which like the other concepts of gospel literacy—call-and-response, bearing witness and acknowledging the burden—is part of the refusal to submit to the burdens of history. As I discuss in later chapters, Citizenship School participants aggressively drew on a tradition of using their own intellectual power to make change happen.

2

"Gonna Lay Down My Burdens": Jim Crow to Composition Studies—A Diagrammatic Perspective

All of the songs were inspirational. All of the songs had one purpose, and that was to reach deep into the moments of our deepest anguish and to say, "We've had worse than this, we can endure."

Harry Belafonte, *Soundtrack for a Revolution* (Guttentag and Sturman)

Those who have no record of what their forebears have accomplished lose the inspiration, which comes from the teaching of biography and history.

Carter G. Woodson, *The Mis-education of the Negro*

FOR MOST OF US HISTORY, SEGREGATION WAS the law. It was a social system meant to keep black and white people apart. By custom and by law, most black people were laborers, servants, and tenant farmers. Black children went to separate, poorer schools and lived in separate, poorer housing. Make no mistake; segregation was the context for black lives throughout the country, but it was practiced more overtly in the South. Segregation had its rules and southern blacks knew that if they didn't obey them—if they didn't step aside to let a white man pass, or if a black man looked too closely at a white woman—the system would be enforced through violence. Groups like the Ku Klux Klan used terrorist tactics to uphold white supremacy and were an ever-present symbol of intimidation. Timothy Tyson, in his book *Radio Free Dixie*, explains the exact nature of Jim Crow. His aesthetic choices so accurately capture the sentiment of the era that he is worth quoting at length:

The power of white skin in the Jim Crow south was both stark and subtle. White supremacy permeated daily life so deeply that most people could no more ponder it than a fish might discuss the wetness of water. Racial etiquette was at once bizarre, arbitrary, and nearly inviolable in what W. E. B. DuBoise termed "the cake of custom." A white man who would never shake hands with a black man would refuse to permit anyone but a black man to shave his face, cut his hair, or give him a shampoo. A white man might share his bed with a black woman but never his table. Black breasts could suckle white babies, black hands would pat out biscuit dough for white mouths, but black heads must not try on a hat in a department store, lest it be rendered unfit for sale to white people. Black maids washed the bodies of the aged and infirm, but the uniforms that they were required to wear could never be laundered in the same washing machines that white people used. While it was permissible to call a favored black man "Uncle" or "Professor"—a mixture of affection and mockery—he must never hear the words "mister" or "sir." Black women were "girls" until they were old enough to be called "auntie," but they could never hear a white person, regardless of age, address them as "Mrs." or "Miss." Whites regarded black people as inherently lazy and shiftless, but when a white man said he had "worked like a nigger," he meant that he had engaged in dirty, back-breaking labor to the point of collapse. (20–21)

What does it mean to recognize an adversity as one's own truth? How is one empowered to attribute value to a liability? By what processes and conditions is one motivated to understand and value past suffering as a source of pride and honor? One of the first lessons most students of composition learn is that writing possesses a cluster of attributes that correspond to certain powerful learning strategies, and that the most successful learners (writers) are those who understand the heuristic role of writing. This lesson was never more visible than in the relationship between the gospel concept of acknowledging the burden and literacy activism. A gospel literacy recognizes that within the history of the suffering of African American people, there is an uplifting refrain of undeniable, unshakable courage. Tyson describes the deeply held belief in America's mind, heart, soul, and experiences that white skin carried power, so eliciting activism with social and persuasive intent in the interest of changing segregationist customs required multiple battles in the war on both African American and white consciousness.

World War II had an immense impact on black hopes for change although the battle for equality was still long and hard. Black Americans fought and died in a segregated US Army. But in Europe they were exposed to a larger unsegregated world and experienced power as some were trained as officers and specialists. Black soldiers returned home with a new sense of themselves. However, the nation they came back to was determined to resist change and ignore African American demands for justice. Then, in the early 1950s, after years of carefully planned litigation, the NAACP brought these demands to the US Supreme Court. The test cases were set in schools, and on May 17, 1954, the Supreme Court ruled unanimously in *Brown v. Board of Education* that segregated schools were unconstitutional, calling into question the whole system of segregation.

Jim Crow was a social system designed to keep black and white people apart. African American people were still considered socially and intellectually inferior and therefore were required to show deference to white people in public spaces: adults were treated like children required to obey their parents. The overwhelming justification for relegating black people to subhuman positions was the belief that they were, by and large, illiterate. And illiteracy was considered a social, emotional, or psychological disability. There is a body of scholarly concentration on the ideology of using literacy to support racial bigotry. Catherine Prendergast jump-starts the most recent conversation by arguing that one of the key components of the "ideology of literacy" rests in the notion that literacy *belongs* to white people (*Literacy* 5). In fact, not until the middle of the twentieth century with the *Brown* decision did we begin to see the demise of prevailing US education policies that enforced laws preserving educational access for whites (16). Consequently, the greatest influence of the *Brown* decision was on the black community. African American people had finally been validated by the highest court in America. The decision emboldened black communities en masse to demand their "inalienable" constitutional rights. Keep in mind that there had always been black people fighting against segregation. In fact, many ministers preached equality, and black unions and organizations such as the Brotherhood of Sleeping Car Porters, the Niagara Movement, and the NAACP all worked consistently for decades to eradicate Jim Crow through speeches, demonstrations, and court cases.

The relentless social activism and advocacy taking place during the Jim Crow era provides a context for illuminating two crucial literacy perspectives, one general and one context specific. First, the evolution of disenfranchisement depended on withholding access to literacy. Second, the inception of the South Carolina Sea Islands Citizenship Schools was directly motivated by the understanding, in the gospel sense, that the power to break free of segregation's intellectual straightjacket lay in overcoming oppressive tradition through literacy. Citizenship Schools represent how, in the mid-twentieth century, African Americans consciously drew on successful intellectual practices integral to African American Sea Islands life. This meant actively pursuing literate goals as a means of combating a racist American institution that deliberately and systematically designed tactics meant to disenfranchise black Americans.

MAPPING THE BURDEN: A HISTORICAL OVERVIEW

In the opening epigraph, Harry Belafonte eloquently declares that African American people embodied the relationship between purpose, power, history, and inherent racist brutality. One of the most resilient traditions protesting this brutality was music. African Americans used the liberators' shelter of music not just to comment on their plight but to resist oppression. Frequently during the Civil Rights era, the song "Down by the Riverside" (known to most as "Gonna Lay Down My Burden") was heard during marches, sit-ins, and mass rallies. "Riverside" is an anthem dating back to the Civil War, when freed slaves trusted that pondering, evaluating, or battling slavery's heavy customs had finally passed and the future held the promise of peace, freedom, and equality. The full emotional thrust comes in the last chorus: "Gonna shake hands around the world, down by the riverside . . . and study war no more." Escaping the burden of historical captivity and making a seamless transition into a protest anthem, "Riverside" embodies the rhetorical goals and strategies of the Civil Rights Movement. Most would see these lyrics as evoking desperate negative energy. But activists hold that singing was an important rhetorical outlet, giving them opportunities to express emotion and encourage emotional involvement in the movement while fostering a heightened sense of spirituality. Gospel singer Mavis Staples describes an alternative perspective of a burden. Explaining its uplifting power, Staples asserts, "If somebody's burdened down and having a hard time, if they're depressed, gospel music will help them. We were singing about freedom. We were singing about when we will be paid for the work we've done" (Guttentag and Sturman). Ultimately, strength is in the burden, and the force of the burden dictates and energizes patterns of African American activism.

Most useful to this discussion is the perspective of a burden as power through literacy activism. I claim this in light of what Fredric Jameson calls "cognitive mapping," recovering and examining some of the material as well as ideological systems from which the South Carolina Sea Islands Citizenship Schools emerged (348). Donna Strickland, in her book *The Managerial Unconscious in the History of Composition Studies*, initiates the use of cognitive mapping within revisionist histories, demonstrating how it is a means for providing "a spatial analysis of culture" (21). Drawing from Strickland, who quotes Jameson, we can understand that cognitive mapping lends itself to an interpretation of the ways in which material conditions—in this case, Sea Islands culture—generate "a type of space unique" to those conditions. In other words, what follows is a spatial diagram or distribution of both the Jim Crow era and composition studies. Ultimately, cognitive mapping is a means of situating gospel literacy within a vaster, often unrepresentable totality, corresponding with the functions of a gospel consciousness.

Literacy activism, then, gets taken up by Sea Islands Citizenship School participants as a defense against racism, a means of exercising autonomy while simultaneously minimizing degrading and often life-threatening situations. Literacy researchers like Harvey Graff (*Labyrinths, Literacy*) have identified literacy acquisition as a "myth," a purely ideological key to economic opportunity, moral growth, and financial security.[1] The truth is that for many African Americans literacy acquisition was this and more: it was a means of staying alive and above ground. During the Jim Crow era, the inability to understand, evaluate, or communicate restrictive notices such as "Negro Waiting Room," "Whites Only," or "Colored Entrance" was more than an ideology or an abstract notion. Under these conditions, not knowing how to interpret these messages could have more than *mythical* consequences.

Armed with a gospel ideology, black registered voters, ready for "battle," participated in Citizenship Schools. They were inspired by the knowledge of a strong tradition of overcoming overwhelming the obstacles of humiliation, frustration, and fear. Alice Wine and other Citizenship School participants clearly understood educational oppression. However, while the burden of Jim Crow weighed heavily on African American people, they aggressively exercised the autonomy to choose their response to this burden, a response that included gospel lyrics as conceptual practice. Wine clarifies how she reconciled burdens with literacy activism:

> The older people sang "I will Overcome" because they had a hard time. They had to row boat to go to the city and carry their peas and corn and potatoes, rice and things. They had a hard time, living and raising their children. Them people had a hard time, living and raising their children. Them people had to work with their children on their back. Rebeltime people were mean. But God changed those people. That's just God. He doing walk knock-kneed. Those oldtime foreparents was something else, I tell you. And one of these days they were able to overcome. They were able to buy the land. Money was scarce, but they had a chance to pay a dollar or

two dollars for a piece of ground. (qtd. in Carawan and Carawan, *Ain't You Got* 207)

All of the songs were inspirational and served the purpose of reaching into the moments of deepest anguish to say, "We've had worse than this, we can endure" if we keep our "eyes on the prize." Ultimately, African American people stepped out of overwhelming circumstances using literacy activism to turn a liability into a lesson—or a burden into a blessing.

Over time, then, literacy became a cornerstone of African American history and culture. For example, even though the "whites only" primary was struck down by the US Supreme Court in the mid-1940s, southern states devoted considerable energy to beefing up electoral roadblocks in subsequent years. Voter registration laws effectively intimidated, confused, and discouraged black people from trying to vote. In South Carolina, those attempting to register had to be able to read any random section of the state constitution, answer twenty-one questions covering everything from civic knowledge to how many beans were in a jar, and provide supporting documentation declaring their place of residence.

The battle against literacy oppression required intellectual weapons or a methodological bomb that became a means of flipping Jim Crow ideology on its head, primarily by fighting the attitude that deemed African American literacy traditions a liability. As a gospel literacy concept, acknowledging the burden operates from the premise that admitting a hardship requires making meaning through a process of access, evaluation, acceptance, and communication located within a historical continuum in which practitioners eagerly participate.[2] Although racist oppression was clearly a *liability,* black people aggressively acted on the *ability* to choose their response. Esau Jenkins explains the value of recognizing the past and its hardships by noting that

some of us, because we can read a little bit more, forget about the place we came from and some of the songs which motivate us to go on. I remember an old woman who worked on a plantation all her life. Some days she would look up at the sun and sing "nobody know the trouble I've seen" or "I been in the storm so long." When older folks have sung those songs, it helped them realize they're trusting in God and reaching for a better day.

Regardless of how well a person can sing the classical songs or opera, they don't have that feeling of people who sang from oppressed soul and need. Those songs come from the soul. Even if it was the blues, it's sweet because it comes from a person that is in need for something and is longing for decency and friendship. Now if we hide those sweet songs and try to get away from what we came from, what will we tell our children about the achievement we have made and the distance we have come? (qtd. in Carawan and Carawan, *Sing* 237)

Sea Islands activists understood that ignoring or minimizing difficult cultural traditions would have adverse consequences on future generations. Conceptualizing a literacy perspective as part of acknowledging the burden is a process of making meaning by accessing an awareness of intellectual ancestry and activism, which in turn gets fertilized through the acquisition of knowledge about political, social, and cultural traditions and history. Ultimately, both *burden* in the everyday sense and *burden* in the gospel sense are ways of knowing, encapsulated through and motivated by the recognition and understanding of both individual and collective intellectual ancestry.[3] Thus, literacy activism takes place at the intersection of power in knowledge and cultural wisdom.

THE PORT ROYAL EXPERIMENT: KNOWLEDGE IS POWER

South Carolina was one of the first states to pass an implicit voter literacy test; in 1890 other southern states began to adopt similar voter tests. South Carolina's literacy test, adopted in 1882, was known as the "eight-box" ballot. Voters were required to place ballots for separate offices in separate boxes. A ballot for the governor's race placed in the box for the Senate seat would be thrown out. To prevent illiterate voters from being coached ahead of time, the order of the boxes was continuously shuffled. The adoption of the "secret ballot" constituted an implicit literacy test, since it prohibited anyone unable to read or write from casting a vote. The power of white skin prevailed, however, as the practice was eliminated when illiterate white people realized that they too were being disenfranchised. In an effort to placate them, southern states adopted an "understanding clause" and a "grandfather clause," which entitled white male voters who could not pass the literacy test to vote provided they could demonstrate their *understanding* of a passage in the state constitution to the satisfaction of the white male registrar, or provided they were related to someone eligible to vote in 1867—the year before black men attained the vote.[4] Discriminatory practices enacted through the "understanding clause" ensured that African Americans would not be eligible to vote.[5]

In the fall of 1865, a group of black men took charge of their burden, gathering at the Zion Church in Charleston, South Carolina, for the purpose of protesting a political convention controlled by white Southerners, many of whom were former slave owners who had surrendered in battles against the Union. During the white convention, they adopted a South Carolina Constitution, which declared that although black men were no longer enslaved, neither were they free citizens and thus could be denied civil rights; primarily, black people were denied the basic services or resources that whites enjoyed. This declaration prompted the South Carolina black men's convention to immediately pass an education-based resolution:

> Whereas, "Knowledge is power" and educated and intelligent people can neither be held in, nor reduced to slavery; Therefore [be it] resolved, That we will insist upon the establishment of good schools for the thorough education of our children through the State; that, to this end, we will contribute freely and liberally of our means, and will earnestly and persistently urge forward every measure calculated to elevate us to the rank of a wise and, enlightened and Christian people. Resolved, That we solemnly urge the parents and guardians

of the young and rising generation, the sad recollection of our forced ignorance and degradation in the past, and by the bright and inspiring hopes of the future, to see that schools are at once established in every neighborhood. (qtd. in Holt 91)

In this passage, the use of quotation marks around the phrase "Knowledge is power" demonstrates that the Zion Church men convened not only to consider the importance of education but also to capture the cultural values held within the body of historical facts gathered through study, observation, and experience. They clearly understood the value of the ideas inferred from the facts of their history, their place in that history, and ultimately, their purpose in the world.

In the gospel tradition, historical knowledge empowers activism. Long before Citizenship Schools were established, the Sea Islands were part of a region in which a large concentration of African Americans had orchestrated major episodes in the struggle for black liberation, starting as far back as the colonial period. Historical research on slave rebellions almost always includes an incident that took place September 9, 1739, when approximately twenty black people met near the Stono River, which borders Wadmalaw and Johns Islands, to organize what became known as the Stono Uprising (Parish, *Slavery: Many Faces* 5–18). This South Carolina insurrection involved up to one hundred enslaved Africans and resulted in the death of sixty captives. Stono fueled already growing white fears of slave rebellion, prompting the Negro Act of 1740, which not only tightened travel and assembly restrictions on African people but also limited the acquisition of literacy. Proving that resisting white power was a consistent regional effort, in 1822 one of the most famous and carefully planned rebellions took place in Charleston under the leadership of a free black man named Denmark Vesey. Unfortunately, the plan was discovered, resulting in the hanging of thirty-five free black Americans and a new round of repressive legislation aimed specifically at African Americans.[6] The freedom struggle continued in South Carolina, when in 1892 David Walker, a former slave, wrote *Walker's Appeal,* which became more than a tool to foster resistance to racial brutality; it was considered a central text in African American reading clubs (McHenry 251).

A crucial literacy initiative that served as a legacy for the Citizenship Schools was the Port Royal Experiment. In February 1862, during the Civil War, Port Royal Island, fifty miles south of Charleston, became the scene of an experiment in literacy freedom that foreshadowed the conflicts of Reconstruction. The Sea Islands had fallen into Union hands, and soon a small group of Northern missionaries and businessmen, including Charlotte Forten Grimke, joined more than 10,000 newly freed captives to start schools, occupying abandoned plantations. Educational historian John R. Rachal explains how Northern newspapers, eager to proclaim African American inferiority, predicted the failure of these efforts (460). However, proving that education changes when people take history into their own hands, Grimke's journals explain that the island's African American "inhabitants" experienced substantial intellectual advances as they grappled with the challenges of history, civics, education, wage labor, and landownership.

STEP BY STEP: A HISTORICAL OVERVIEW FROM JOHNS ISLAND TO HIGHLANDER FOLK SCHOOL

Following the Civil War, one of the benefits of Reconstruction was that African American men on the four islands—James, Johns, Wadmalaw, and Edisto—could legally vote. The triumph of white supremacy, however, effectively froze them out of political participation. Politically disempowered, black American island residents continued to work hard to attain and maintain economic independence. Sam Gadsden, an Edisto Island cotton farmer in the early 1900s, was able to make a living as a cotton farmer even though he was paid substantially less for his crop than his white counterparts were. Taking advantage of the island's geographical isolation, Gadsden took charge of the situation, manipulating his economic vulnerability by selling his cotton to several white merchants (see Payne).

Isolation, often considered a liability, actually contributed to the success of the Citizenship Schools on the Sea Islands. Much as in African American sacred spaces, few whites were present to oppose the learning initiatives taking place. Isolation, as a geographical theme, impacted the course of Sea Islands history in the way people lived and their quality of life. In 1950 the majority of the Sea Islands population was descended from former slaves who had worked on huge rice and cotton plantations. After the Civil War, through white flight, many black residents obtained ownership of small farms on one to twenty-five acres, raising vegetables and cotton. The preservation of Gullah language and culture is the ultimate benefit of isolation. Johns Island, the site of the first school, is located sixteen miles south of Charleston. The isolation eased in 1950 when the first bridge was built connecting the islands to the mainland. Before the bridges were built, Johns Island residents who wanted access to Charleston had to take a nine-hour boat ride.

In 1951, Esau Jenkins, a Johns Island resident, operated a transportation service between the Islands and Charleston. He used his transportation business as an opportunity to help people memorize portions of the South Carolina Constitution for the voter registration test. Jenkins was profoundly self-sufficient, forging collective solutions to oppressive burdens. He came up with the idea for the Sea Islands adult literacy initiative while attending a workshop at the Highlander Folk School. (For more on Highlander, see the following section.)

In 1953, Highlander sponsored a series of workshops in which black and white Americans discussed and developed programs centered on school desegregation and human rights. These workshops were proactive responses to the *Brown v. Board of Education* Supreme Court decision. From these workshops, Highlander became increasingly involved in the Civil Rights Movement. One of its most significant contributions to the movement was the establishment of the South Carolina Sea Islands Citizenship Schools, which sought to help African American residents meet the requirements for South Carolina voter registration. Citizenship School organizers Septima Clark, Bernice Robinson, Myles Horton, and Esau Jenkins wrote a report to expand the program titled "A Proposal for the Citizenship School Training Program," in which they attribute the success of the Citizenship Schools primarily to what organizers identified as "the immediacy of the era" (Highlander Folk School, "Proposal").[7] In 1957 barriers to voter registration were vital to white supremacy throughout the South. For example, in South Carolina only 17.4 percent of eligible African Americans were registered (Mintz and Price 1, 7, 29). The Sea Islands Citizenship Schools were responsible for a 100 percent increase in African American voter registration. Highlander's 1959–1960 quarterly reports show that 182 adults enrolled in Citizenship School classes on Promise Land (the northern section of Johns Island). On the islands of Wadmalaw, Edisto, and North Charleston, 65 African Americans became registered voters. The official reports show that by March 1960 there were 200 registered African American voters on Edisto Island, up from 40 in 1958. The reports are not as specific for Johns Island; they simply document without specific numbers that African American voters on Johns Island increased by 300 percent from 1956 to 1960. In 1960–1961 (December–February), records indicate that classes held in North Charleston, Edisto, and Wadmalaw saw 100 out of 111 African American Citizenship School participants become registered voters (see also Tjerandsen 167–68; Glen).[8]

Indicative of a burden ideology, participation in the Citizenship Schools was fueled by the failed attempts of the local and federal governments to sponsor adult literacy initiatives for African Americans. The failure of government-sponsored programs was inherent in their weak curriculum design. Bernice Robinson, the first Citizenship School teacher, credits the success of the Sea Islands program to the judgment and understanding of past practices that ended in failure:

> The direction and substance of a program must merge *from* the people and not [be] *brought* to them, however well intentioned. This is what is called the "percolator effect" rather than the "drip" technique. If a program is to work the people must have the power of making decisions about what they want to do. (Oldendorf Interview)[9]

The Sea Islands tradition of self-sufficiency, coupled with a basic tenet of the Highlander philosophy, resonate with the gospel concept of acknowledging the burden. Myles Horton concludes that "'oppressed people know the answer to their own problems'" (qtd. in Morris 142). Underlying this philosophy is a fundamental belief in the dignity, life knowledge, intellectual competence, and capacity for growth possessed by adult learners, regardless of the level of reading, writing, or other academic experience. This is a crucial philosophy, separating the Citizenship Schools from previous unsuccessful efforts to teach African American adults on the Sea Islands. When the Charleston County Public Schools attempted to initiate literacy programs, facilitators often appeared insensitive to aspects of Sea Islands culture—like the requirements of planting season—as well as disinterested in participants' literacy acquisition motives. Although the superintendent commissioned a public school teacher in addition to classrooms, a major problem arose when adults who were tall or overweight could not sit comfortably on chairs designed for six-year-old children. Horton, in consultation with Sea Islands residents, was aware of these attempts as they designed the Sea Islands program. Historian Frank Adams explains:

> Gradually, he [Horton] learned that the islanders were ill at ease in the state's adult literacy program for some very simple, but not so obvious reasons. For one thing, the adults didn't fit into the classroom chairs. They'd been designed for children. Not only were the adults who attended uncomfortable, but they were called "Daddy Long-legs," and there was just enough deprecation in the nickname to cause embarrassment, just enough embarrassment to cause a prideful man or woman to quit. In just the same way, they were being taught as children: step-by-step; a-b-c-d; "the ball is red"; "New York is a big city." They were being asked to delay reading sentences useful to them until they could read sentences of dubious value to children. It seemed very far from the Constitution. The few who had enrolled just stopped going to classes. (*Unearthing* 512)

The obvious burden here is humiliation. The organizers of the Citizenship Schools—Clark, Horton, Robinson, and Jenkins—took action by designing a program in which adult learners were treated as capital *A* Adult learners.

Government-sanctioned efforts to provide learning opportunities made no effort to ease feelings of inferiority. Ultimately, these practices were both physically and emotionally abusive. Participants were physically assaulted by having to endure the discomfort of forcing their adult bodies into children's desks, abuse compounded by an irrelevant curriculum designed for children. The teachers, commissioned by the public school system, used the same readiness and primer reading materials that were ordinarily used for first- through third-grade children—and organizers were unwilling to entertain alternate curriculum choices. This was the case regardless of academic level. African American adults were not interested in the world of "Dick and Jane." Bernice Robinson explains how humiliation played a part in the failure of previous attempts to establish adult education programs:

> They'd had adult classes many times in the public schools. Every year they opened it up in three public schools. They'd start off with a big enrollment and in about a month's time, it just fizzled out. They were teaching them just like they would be teaching kids. (Oldendorf Interview)

Even adult education programs that did not humiliate students in the manner Bernice Robinson describes were unable to equal the success of the Citizenship Schools. For instance, starting in 1931 and working with the help of Wil Lou Gray, a woman named Miss Gregory tutored African Americans on Edisto Island with limited results. Cognizant of the failure of this and other adult education classes sponsored by the Charleston County School Board, Citizenship School organizers knew that a night school for adults would have to be located outside the traditional schoolroom and in a setting familiar to adults—or, as Horton put it, "'the work of learning to read and write had to be adult work'" (qtd. in Adams, *Unearthing* 226). In addition, they needed to put educational programs where the people lived and to let them decide what they wanted to learn. Therefore, the first school on Johns Island was held in the back of a general store that was owned by a local organization called the Progressive Club.[10] Finally, everyone agreed that it was important for the teachers to come from the community. They needed to be people who understood the culture, who could communicate with the residents, and who were respected and recognized by the participants. But teachers also had to have been to Highlander Folk School and to know Highlander's philosophy (Robinson, Thrasher and Wigginton Interview, Oldendorf Interview).

SEEDS OF FIRE: THE HIGHLANDER FOLK SCHOOL

The idea that the direction of the Citizenship Schools must come from "the people" was no coincidence. Embedded in the consciousness of accepting the burden is the belief that "we don't choose our burdens, but we surely can choose our response to them," a foundational philosophy resonating of the Highlander Folk School. Established by Myles Horton and Don West in 1932 in the Cumberland Mountains near Monteagle, Tennessee, the school was founded primarily to focus on the Appalachian labor movement.[11] However, Highlander's focus on human rights issues, specifically segregation, intensified during the 1950s and 1960s. Because of Highlander's involvement in the Civil Rights Movement, which included facilitating community-organizing workshops, the state of Tennessee revoked its charter and confiscated its property. Horton, anticipating this action, secured another charter in a different name, Highlander Research and Education Center, moving to Knoxville, Tennessee, in 1961. The focus shifted back to the Appalachian people in 1971 after the center moved to its current location in New Market, located in the mountains near Knoxville.

Administrative control of Citizenship Schools was given to the Southern Christian Leadership Conference (SCLC) in 1961 because of a temporary injunction by the State of Tennessee to close the Monteagle center. Rare for this time was the mixing of races, but during Highlander's workshops, both black and white Americans participated. Race mixing, one of white segregationists' greatest fears, prompted the state's attorney general to padlock Highlander's doors. Horton refused to stop the literacy crusade and simply shifted management of the Citizenship Schools to the SCLC. This was a natural transition primarily because the radical Christian philosophies of Horton's mentor, Reinhold Niebuhr, had a strong influence on Martin Luther King Jr., who led the SCLC. Niebuhr was a socialist Christian who guided Horton's commitment to human rights activism. Frank Adams, author of *Unearthing Seeds of Fire: The Idea of Highlander*, a book on Highlander and Horton's life and activism, describes Niebuhr's influence by stating that "he used Marxism to criticize liberal social Christianity[,] declaring himself a socialist, or socialist Christian Marxist" (12). Niebuhr identified capitalism as "an expression of a dying civilization" (12). Both King's and Horton's primary attraction was to Niebuhr's theology and defense of working people, an idea Horton followed when developing Highlander programs. During a news conference, he told reporters, "'You can padlock a building. But you can't padlock an idea. Highlander is an idea. You can't kill it and you can't close it in. This workshop is part of the idea. It will grow wherever people take it'" (qtd. in Adams, *Unearthing* 133).

In 1961, when Highlander gave administrative control of the Citizenship Schools to the SCLC, the program's focus shifted from primarily basic literacy acquisition to "first-class citizenship" and voter registration programs. Although basic literacy instruction continued, for the SCLC mission first-class citizenship was the core purpose. To their credit, they broadened the scope of the literacy endeavor from a few hundred disenfranchised people on the Sea Islands of South Carolina to several thousand people all over the Deep South. While the personalized spirit of the program dimmed, people continued to register to vote. As part of the transformation, the name of the program changed several times, from Highlander Citizenship Schools to the Citizenship Education Program to the more popular Freedom Schools. Transitioning from the initial Sea Islands trajectory, where learners were teachers (or each-one-teach-one), the SCLC required that teachers complete application forms and include experience and references. The program's switch from the Citizenship Education Program to Freedom Schools served as a segue for many legendary activists to join the Civil Rights Movement, including Andrew Young, Dorothy Cotton, Fannie Lou Hamer, and Julian Bond.[12] Ultimately, the Freedom Schools were responsible for enrolling more than 50,000 registered voters. Meanwhile, Highlander continued Civil Rights educational activities and worked closely with such groups as the Student Nonviolent Coordinating Committee (SNCC), the Congress of Racial Equality (CORE), and the Council of Federated Organizations (CFO).[13] This was all possible because funding for Highlander was a minimal concern due to a sizable donation from the Schwartzhaupt Foundation.[14] In 1953, Highlander received a $44,000 grant for the purpose of developing programs to train local community-based leaders. In the end, one of Highlander's most successful and visible projects was the South Carolina Sea Islands Citizenship Schools, Highlander's primary focus between 1958 and 1965.

3

"I Got Some Pride": Call-and-Response as an Intellectual Principle of Literacy Acquisition and Use

ON AUGUST 6, 1954, BERNICE ROBINSON attended a weeklong workshop at Highlander Folk School. The topic was "World Problems, the United Nations, and You," a theme reflecting Highlander's interest in creating solidarity between African Americans' social justice crusades and global social justice movements. Septima Clark and Esau Jenkins also attended this workshop. Toward the conclusion of the sessions, as Robinson explains, the facilitator initiated a series of questions—a call—asking: "What are we going to do when we get back home? How are we going to transmit our experiences this week back in our community? How are we going to promote the United Nations when we get back to Charleston and other places?" Esau Jenkins responded: "I don't know anything about promoting the United Nations, but I'll tell you what I would like to promote!"[1] He went on to advocate for a Sea Islands literacy program focused on voter registration. In effect, Jenkins responded by initiating a new call, emphasizing the high levels of illiteracy in his community and the need for reading and writing instruction. Jenkins's reaction included a goal directly advocating for Johns Island residents, conveying *their* expressed desire to learn to read and write.

By most accounts, Esau Jenkins gets credit for initiating the Citizenship School idea. He did this by calling or announcing a need, grounded in individual and shared literacy experiences. And while this initial exchange provides a basic introduction to the motives behind the establishment of the Citizenship Schools, we are left with questions about what motivated the leadership practices and organizing strategies and how participants drew from a call-and-response ideology.

Septima Clark and Bernice Robinson were also first responders, participating in the initial Citizenship School call. At the same time, they were also operating within an African American tradition that identifies literate members of the community as those primarily responsible for the survival and advancement of the community as a whole. Jenkins executed call-and-response, a culturally informed approach to literacy action, propelling the Citizenship School literacy crusade into action.

Esau Jenkins was both a Citizenship School teacher and a learner. Most important, he is an example of a community leader who took the responsibility of initiating teaching and learning into his own hands. Before the first official Highlander-sponsored citizenship education class, Jenkins used his transportation service, a bus, as a classroom to teach people to read the section of the South Carolina Constitution needed to pass the voting registration literacy test. He did this while driving Johns Island residents across bridges to work in Charleston.

Even after the bridges were built, the Sea Islands remained culturally insulated. Agriculture remained the primary income source on the islands, and one consequence of its geographical separation was the magnification of oppressive living conditions. George Kearney, a white sociologist and Highlander staff member, visited the Sea Islands in 1955 and reported that most African American farmers were required to sell their produce through middlemen. Many farmers were cheated out of fair exchange because they had limited or no math and reading skills (Oldendorf, "Literacy" 36).

Jenkins witnessed residents harvesting the land for generations while accepting the reality of being unable to do the things that only registered voters could accomplish.[2] He was aware that the survival and advancement of the community depended on getting black people both registered and voting. This strategy required that they pass a voting literacy test. These exams were the result of the failure of Reconstruction in 1895, giving rise to literacy tests that were specifically designed and implemented for the disenfranchisement of African Americans. There was no uniformity to them; the tests were often designed and administered at the whim of the voting registrar on duty at any given time. The test was usually based on the ability to read and interpret a section of the South Carolina Constitution. Traditionally, only African American residents were required to take these tests. But this was not the only obstacle. Other voting laws included grandfather clauses, white primaries, and poll taxes. Jenkins was motivated by the belief that the solution to easing discrimination lay in valuing education. He stated that "standing for the right has always been education" (Carawan and Carawan, *Ain't You Got* 140). This is a motto he applied to himself, his children (he sent seven to college), and his community.

Jenkins amped up his voting rights campaign even though his reading and writing aptitude equaled that of most of the people he was teaching. However, he eagerly improved on his fourth-grade education while attempting to teach. Describing his formal education, Jenkins explains how self-motivation was a rule and not an option:

> I haven't gotten any further than the fourth grade in grammar school here. I had to work, and because of that I had to leave school. And then too, the school we had here wasn't encouraging to go to. We had around fifty children and one teacher with a one-door school. (qtd. in Carawan and Carawan, *Ain't You Got* 142)

Black children were required to hurdle the Charleston Department of Education's perpetuation of psychological obstacles for those with an intense desire to learn. Jenkins held onto vivid memories of being a black child required to attend a school that was painted black. This was done in a conscious effort to reinforce the idea that this was the place for black children. Along with the overcrowded environment, this dirty tactic was just the motivation the adult Jenkins needed. Such treatment fostered in him a critically conscious viewpoint, one determined to reclaim the souls of his people, to focus their energies toward change, and to inspire them to be bold.

He explains that "it discouraged me when I got some pride. I went to Charleston and started working on a boat" (142). But Jenkins's responsibilities increased after he married, reviving his decision to continue his education. He worked days and went to night school while at the same time holding literacy classes on his bus.

Among his motives for such intense participation in literacy acquisition were the economic limits stemming from language differences. However, the solution to this obstacle was to learn modern Greek, the language of most of Charleston's shop owners and the people he needed to trade with. Jenkins explains that he observed the Greek merchants' purchasing power and the money they spent on goods, claiming, "So I thought the best thing for me to do then is to try to learn the Greeks' language." He studied Greek and in two years was buying and trading with them. He notes that it took enormous effort to be able to understand the Greek language in everyday conversation (Carawan and Carawan, *Ain't You Got* 145). Jenkins's attitude and beliefs about language and learning are not just values he used in his community leadership activities—he passed these values on to his children. He explains that a benefit of speaking Greek was that it "helped me to transact my own business, and now I'm happy to say that I was able to have my children educated. One son is a captain in the Army, one a navigator in the Air Force, two daughters are teaching, one son is a professor of music" (142–43). Jenkins has transferred his individual passion for literacy learning to promote the survival and growth of the community and proudly proclaims, "And now there are other folks on this island being encouraged to send their children to get a higher education. We know that some day in the near future Johns Island will be a better place to live" (143).

Jenkins is not merely illustrating simple economic survival; he is also enacting literacy that brings about social and economic security. His rise to leadership also exposes a critical intelligence rarely attached to "basic" literacy. His capacity for knowledge demonstrates his reflective, attentive consideration of larger systems in a particular time and place.

Literacy and language permeate Jenkins's path toward becoming a community leader, and his account reveals the practices, meanings, and value of literacy for ordinary, grassroots people. As he relates, Jenkins and his family gained economic and social benefits as a result of teaching and learning to read and write. However, he remained concerned about the survival and success of his community. He spoke, for example, about inadequate housing and health care, which he equated with inadequate learning opportunities. The difficulty in obtaining a high school education was magnified by the reality that the school for the black children on the island was separate and unequal, as in similar schools throughout the United States. Jenkins stressed that "the white kids were riding in school buses and the buses were warm" while the black children had to walk five to ten miles to their school (Carawan and Carawan, *Ain't You Got* 153).[3] Sea Islands children were also required to wait in the snow or rain for the teacher, who might or might not show up from Charleston. When the teacher arrived, the children had to collect firewood to warm the schoolhouse. Jenkins was concerned about the ability of the children to concentrate under these circumstances, claiming that the school for black children had one teacher for forty to fifty children "to carry 'em from scratch to seventh grade" (154). These conditions not only motivated Jenkins's campaign for communal survival, but they also fueled his leadership drive. In 1945 he organized other residents to remedy the education problems by purchasing a bus to transport his and others' children to the high school for African American children in Charleston. And in 1953, he initiated the campaign to open Haut Gap High School on Johns Island, the first for African American students (Oldendorf, "Highlander" 59).

By all accounts, a response that simultaneously affirms and changes the direction of a call is nonabrasive; it doesn't refuse to go along with the call. A response that resists dominant social forces denotes deeper thinking, reasoning, and expression: intellectual work. However, resisting here doesn't mean refusing to accept an idea but instead having the good sense to hold off while acknowledging a new verse. Jenkins did accept the need to promote the United Nations agenda, but he also changed the direction of the agenda, issuing an alternative goal for human rights that included literacy acquisition and use. Participants also engaged in a resistance ideology by refusing to focus teaching and learning practices only on civic or political material. Sea Islands citizens took ownership of the call to activism, seeking autonomy, subjectivity, and identity through literate practices, meanings, and values. Learning became a space where the individual and the group resisted and/or changed preestablished social and political methods and motives. At the same time, call-and-response here became a means to explore individual community-based intellectual practices, meanings, and values of literacy learning. While individual participants asserted a unified desire for learning, they also took control of and changed teaching and learning ideologies, even when those ideologies originated within the group.

Two specific incidents accelerated Jenkins toward initiating the call for the Citizenship Schools. Each event involved a personal reassessment of the relationship between the value of the life of a black man and that of a dog. According to Jenkins, "Two evil things that happened motivated me to get involved in my work on Johns Island" (Carawan and Carawan, *Ain't You Got* 145). A black driver accidentally ran over and killed a white man's dog. The white man, who was not from the island, chased the black man, forcing him to his knees. While the black man begged for his life, the white man shot him. The second incident involved Sammy Grant, a young black boy who was shot by Mr. Malone, a white man from Mississippi, in a dispute over a barking dog. In both cases, the families attempted to access the legal system to obtain justice. Both families hired white lawyers, believing justice could be found through legal action. The courts ignored both cases and nothing was ever done for either family. As a result of these incidents, Jenkins believed that the physical survival of the community literally depended on literacy learning solutions that would lead to social and political autonomy (Oldendorf, "Highlander" 59):

These are the things then, that motivated me to organize in 1949 a progressive movement, that we could help the people to be better citizens, give them a chance to get a better education, and know how to reason and look out for themselves, and take more part in political action. (qtd. in Carawan and Carawan, *Ain't You Got* 145)

After the high school was built on Johns Island, Jenkins used his buses to transport adults from the island to jobs in Charleston. This practice helped cement his leadership position while at the same time drawing support for literacy learning from a captive audience. During the trips to Charleston, he took the opportunity to teach people to read and write the portion of the South Carolina Constitution that he knew needed to be read before black people could register to vote. Jenkins's bus was the initial space for the Johns Island Citizenship Schools. One of his first students and the first to successfully register as a result of his teaching was Alice Wine. She explains her literacy and language experience as follows:

I came around to get registering through Mr. Esau Jenkins. He started to help me read and when I get to them hard words I feel jump it. My tongue so heavy until I couldn't pronounce the words, you know. But he said to me, "No the hard words is the things for you to learn." Then he take me to the registration board on Society Street and we get in line. (qtd. in Carawan and Carawan, *Ain't You Got* 149)

Wine further revealed that she did not learn by decoding and comprehension. Rather, she memorized the reading through oral repetition. Bernice Robinson adds flavor to this event, explaining that while Wine was waiting in line to register, she began to call out words missed by those in line ahead of her:

She memorized it so well, that when she was standing in line to get registered, some people ahead of her if they would miss a word, she would tell them what it was, when she got up to the counter, they didn't even bother her to go and make her read. They just told her "no prompting" "no prompting in here" and they just figured she know it so well, there wasn't any need, they just went on and gave her hers.[4]

Both Robinson and Jenkins knew that memorization would not work for everyone. Further complicating the idea that rote memorization was an impractical solution to illiteracy was Alice Wine's participation in the program even after achieving the civic inclusion of becoming a registered voter. She eventually took up leisure reading, becoming an avid novel reader (Clark, *Echo* 154). Jenkins broadened literacy needs beyond voting rights. For example, Bernice Robinson was an active member of the NAACP, Urban League, and her church, but her move to further literacy action was prompted by Jenkins's initial response to illiteracy. She states:

> And then he talked about the literacy on the islands. Well, you know, [it's] like you say, we accepted the black school, we accepted the whites and the colored fountain as a way of life. I knew that there was a lot of illiteracy all around me, but I accepted that as a fact, that there was nothing you could do about it. That was gonna be there, you know, and there was nothing anybody could do about it. When Esau started talking about it, then, you know, it started to really coming through and something to think about. People can't read, you know. So he turned a whole workshop around; [*laughs*] everybody became interested in this, you know.[5]

In 1954, Jenkins's leadership, community organizing, and teaching efforts placed him in a position to *turn around* a call for human rights activism to a response centered on learning and teaching initiatives. According to Bernice Robinson, the last days of the United Nations workshop became a crusade to set up literacy classes on Johns Island.

In her book *If You Don't Go, Don't Hinder Me: The African American Sacred Song Tradition*, Bernice Reagon carefully explains that for call-and-response to work, the initial call must be issued by a galvanizing, well-organized leader or leaders. She provides an in-depth illustration of how this works in both her audio project *Voices of the Civil Rights Movement* and her book. Reagon emphasizes that the leader is primarily a guide who suggests the direction the group should take, so it is crucial that the leader be an organized, clear thinker. The initial call to Sea Islands residents not only draws attention to those involved in the first steps, but it also relies on specific characteristics of the leadership's organizing skills, which demonstrate coherent thinking, logical reasoning, and lucid expression. Two key call-and-response elements are highlighted within the context of Citizenship School literacy activities: the initial call and the response. Both require a shared history that spreads through each stage of the teaching and learning process. Smitherman's description of call-and-response as a means of teaching is the most useful study for illuminating Sea Islands activism (see especially *Talkin' and Testifyin'* and *Talkin' That Talk*).

Secure in his commitment to the community and his knowledge that literacy was the key to freedom, Jenkins seized the opportunity to ask Myles Horton, Highlander's director, to sponsor adult learning classes. The first call was to attain "better" citizenship through voter registration (Adams, *Unearthing* 113). Acquisition of this right was deeply rooted in the initial call. As we will see later, it became less important within the goals taken up in participants' responses. In addition, demonstrating leadership initiative and advanced planning, Jenkins requested that Myles Horton and his wife, Zilphia, director of the Highlander Music Education program, visit Johns Island. Jenkins used this visit as an opportunity to encourage and secure the Hortons' investment in the literacy teaching he had already begun. Enacting the gospel ritual of call-and-response, Jenkins began the Citizenship Schools with one voice, picking up backup singers along the way: Septima Clark, the Carawans, Ethel Grimball, Anderson Mack, Bernice Robinson, and the Highlander staff. Eventually, the singers became a chorus of the residents of the Sea Islands: Johns, Wadmalaw, Edisto, and Daufuskie. And with harmonious refrain, they aligned with Highlander's primary purpose: to provide a space to organize, encourage, and train community leaders in community organizing, as well as to do literacy education. Printed on a Citizenship Schools flyer is the following statement:

The Citizenship Schools are for adults. Their immediate program is teaching reading and writing. They help students to pass literacy tests for voting. But they also give an all-around education in community development which includes housing, recreation, health, and improved home life. Specific subjects include filing income tax forms, understanding of tax-supported resources such as water testing for wells, aid to handicapped children, public health facilities, how government is run, social security, etc.[6]

Admittedly, voter registration is embedded in these goals, but communal survival was an important motivator in the activities of this literacy learning crusade. Jenkins continued to build his leadership position, demonstrating an organizational aptitude that intersected with language and literacy learning.

TEACHING TO LEARN WHILE LEARNING TO TEACH

Esau Jenkins played a central role in the first steps of the Citizenship Schools. However, we look to Bernice Robinson, the first official Citizenship School teacher, to see how leadership and organizing and teaching and learning interrelate. Robinson, a beautician and tailor by trade, was not only an active participant in the initial call but also took charge of soliciting for funding as well as learners. This was in addition to learning how to prepare and implement teaching activities.

Like Jenkins, Robinson displayed a high level of organizational skill, and she implemented that skill in her teaching so that the practices, meanings, and values of literacy stayed closely connected to breaking down systems of oppression. Robinson's teaching and learning practices as well as her intellectual values were central to her leadership and organizing principles. For example, in a 1980 interview celebrating Highlander's fiftieth anniversary, Robinson discusses how she participated in the initial Citizenship School recruitment efforts. Although Esau Jenkins arranged some of the recruitment meetings, she sustained the efforts independently. When she was asked if Jenkins had helped her with the initial recruiting, Robinson responded:

No, all he did was introduce me to the people. [*laughs*] I went around to churches. Sometimes I went to churches on my own, you know. He set up appointments for me because he was pretty much involved with his church, and every Sunday Esau had something to do. In fact, he ran his church when the minister wasn't there. And the minister wasn't there every Sunday, at his church. But he would set up appointments for me at various churches on the island and I, I knew the people. We had worked and through the NAACP we had worked over there. Highlander had been down there before with different types of workshops, and I had been to all the meetings and stuff over the island. So I really knew the people. It wasn't like I was walking into a strange setup. (Thrasher and Wigginton Interview)

Good organizational skills are an essential characteristic of effective leadership. It is important to note that during this time Robinson was an independent businesswoman, running her own beauty shop[7] and tailoring business. And while this freed her to make the enormous time commitment to the Citizenship Schools, it also saved her from the economic reprisals that others faced when taking official stands against Jim Crow practices. Robinson cultivated her leadership role through her activities in the community. She needed to be well organized. In addition to her social and political activism, Robinson was the primary caregiver to her mother and also the only teacher during the initial stages of the Citizenship Schools:

I was the only teacher; I don't know yet how I did it. . . . So that meant that I cut short my work in the beauty shop in order to finish up, get my mother a light supper, get myself together and get over there [Johns' Island] by 7 o'clock. I would cut back on a lot of my own work, because even my sewing and stuff I would have to do it the nights that I wasn't over there. And the night I wasn't over there, I was trying to plan some lessons to see where I could reach them again in another area of something. (Thrasher and Wigginton Interview)

Her statement reinforces the notion that multitasking—teaching math, reading, writing, and civics and taking care of family and other work obligations—was worth the effort, particularly when she could include political activism in her teaching.

> So, but it was interesting, I got into it and I became so involved with those people that nothing else really mattered. Just to see people making a part of theirselves, 65-year-old women, who finally recognized her name in a bunch of names on the board, meant something to me. It really meant something. The feeling, I could never explain or express, how I felt when I put all those names up on the board and this woman I said to her "Now, can you find your name up there on the board?" "Yes, ma'am, I sure can!" She took the ruler out of my hand: "That's my name there, Annie, A-n-n-i-e, and that's my other name down there, Vastine. V-a-s-t-i-n-e." I had goose pimples all over me. That woman could not read or write when she came in there and she could recognize her name in the short space of time. We only worked two months in the first part of '57, January and February, that's the only two months we could work. (Thrasher and Wigginton Interview)

Robinson expresses the value she placed on her role as a leader and teacher while giving a glimpse into the meaning of literacy learning for others, including the individual value of learning to read and write.

Robinson's leadership philosophy was embedded in her teaching and learning activities—a point she makes during a talk delivered at the Cabrillo Community College Literacy Conference on October 11, 1986:

> Not one of us had ever made the decision to become a leader. But there were problems with which we were confronted, and we made a move to solve them. Although reluctantly. But that is how leaders are born and developed. *You see a problem and you begin to address it—talk it over with others, and soon you find others looking to you for leadership and willing to support you in the effort.* Once a decision is made to do

something, then the next step is to *gather* all the facts relating to that problem—sharing this information with others in your group—requesting suggestions as to how and what way should you tackle the problem. Members of your group, in order to avoid responsibility, may attempt to put the leader in an "expertise position." If as a leader you accept this status and make decisions for the groups, you will lose group support and commitment.[8] (emphasis mine)

Robinson acknowledges the value of a reciprocal relationship—shared communication and knowledge—between the leader and the group. She knows that the individual is essential to the group and vice versa. Studies have shown that shared interaction between the group and the leader is a practice among some African cultures (see Herskovits; Williams-Jones). In addition, most perspectives on African and African American cultural traditions affirm that audience participation is crucial to the gospel experience and that interjections and responses to performers such as "go 'head," "that's right," and "sho' nuff" are frequent practices that act as an emotional catalyst to encourage the leader to continue. Interestingly, in the African storytelling tradition, it is considered rude or impolite to sit silently without response or some appropriate comment. This is a *response* trait that is clearly traceable in accounts of African American sacred and secular situations. One is just as prone to encounter responsive verbal and nonverbal interaction between an individual and the group at a political rally as in a gospel church; passive audience attitudes are Western European aesthetic norms (Reagon, *Voices*).

Although some might observe that *all* leaders interact with the group and that *all* leadership relies to some degree on shared communication and knowledge, in the context of the Citizenship Schools we see this principle operating in a particular time and place because Robinson used it as a means of teaching and learning. Her initial contact with participants as a Citizenship School teacher demonstrates an intersection between her leadership philosophies and organizational strategies, which were also embedded in her teaching and learning practices. For example, when given the responsibility of teaching, she began the process with an initial group discussion in an effort to not only find out learners' expectations for learning but also to explore ways of tackling the problems.

And they came in that [first] night and I told them that they ask me to teach this class. But I'm not going to be the teacher, we gonna learn together. You gonna teach me some things and maybe there are a few things I might be able to teach you. But I don't consider myself a teacher. I just feel that I'm here to learn with you, you know, learn things together.

So I said we're going to work together and we're going to learn from each other. Then I brought them up one by one to find out where they were as far as reading and writing was concerned. Some could read a little bit; some could write a little bit. Some could read all right. I really don't know where I got the ideas from. But I wanted to find out what they wanted to learn. They wanted to learn how to make an order blank for the catalogue, and then they had wanted, of course, to read the Bible. Then they wanted to be able to read so when the children who were living away from home and write them letters they wouldn't have to take it to the white people to read. (Thrasher and Wigginton Interview)

On the one hand, Robinson demonstrates a key principle of the initial call by showing she was organized enough to arrange a clear direction for learning and teaching, which was also a shared responsibility. However, Robinson also rested on her knowledge of how interchangeable roles operate within the principle of call-and-response. Her teaching and learning strategies make it obvious that a good leader is obligated to respond to the call of the group.

Robinson always demonstrates immense humility, explaining that she doesn't know where she got the idea to base her teaching on the individual needs within the group. But in analyzing her early learning experiences, choices, or lack thereof, she explains how she was denied the opportunity to express her literacy needs. Her childhood learning experiences, from seventh through ninth grades, included being forced to take classes in cooking, sewing, and laundry.

The set of courses enforced by school administrators, through the development of a racist and sexist curriculum, denied her a positive learning experience but at the same time formed her learning principles and values. Robinson also had a strong desire to learn music; therefore, being forced to learn a predetermined curriculum did not sit well with her. This teaching and learning philosophy and practice is reflected in her development of the initial Citizenship School curriculum, which included learning to write out postal money orders, mathematics, and sewing. When faced with the dilemma of multiple reading and writing levels as well as age differences among her students, Robinson developed or adapted specific teaching practices based on the expressed needs of the group. She simultaneously demonstrated her pedagogical and her organizational skills, which are crucial to successful leadership. In the midst of all this, she arranged a direction for the intellectual growth of some unexpected young women attending the classes. Robinson was faced with the dilemma of what to do with the daughters of learners who were present in the classes. She demonstrates creative intellectual strategies by thinking through the situation and taking advantage of the tools available to her:

> Now what are you going to do with them? Because they giggled when their parents stumbled over words. You got to do something with them. I don't know yet how I did this, two hours of work each night. I taught the teenagers how to crochet. Then Myles sent me some material on speaking. He sent me some material on speaking. He sent this whole box of stuff. I guess he thought, well, Bernice can use this. And I did. Public speaking. So I came back to the teenagers to study speaking, and I had them to stand up in front of the class and tell us something. Just make a little talk. And they stumbled and we giggled at them. That is how I handled that situation, because naturally the adults were sensitive. (Thrasher and Wigginton Interview)

Her literacy practices are reflected in Robinson's classroom interactions. Her ability to multitask is obvious, along with other essential attributes for a well-organized leader, such as creativity and thinking on her feet. She enters this community with the intention of teaching basic literacy skills but expands her focus to include public speaking and protocol—teaching a life lesson on respect.

Robinson's previous knowledge of Sea Islands culture helped her feel comfortable and able to assume responsibility for her own learning process. She was not bashful or embarrassed that she was not a formally trained teacher, taking comfort in the fact that she was chosen by Clark, Horton, and Jenkins primarily *because* of her lack of traditional teacher training. This, coupled with shared cultural experiences as well as knowing who some of the people were and what they wanted to learn, relieved her nervousness while determining her pedagogical choices.

Robinson's teaching and learning operated within a time and space continuum, secure in a shared history and culture. This is evident in her response to historians' queries about her experience. During most of her recorded documentary interviews, Robinson recalls that she took advantage of opportunities to reinforce her position as a member of the group by emphasizing that, regardless of her being appointed the teacher, they all shared similar educational experiences and goals. They were all there to learn.

Her first night of teaching began with an initial call based on the belief that everyone could learn writing by using primers designed for children. However, Robinson was a perceptive and creative woman who knew from their shared history that she could not teach adults by using inferior materials. The response she felt as soon as she came in contact with individual participants—and sincerely understanding their feelings about reading and writing—led her to resist the initial call, thus changing the response to include texts that local people wanted to learn. In reflecting on this period, Robinson reveals her learning assumptions and reasons for approaching the Citizenship School as a peer:

> I think that sort of settled the folks down, you know, and they—'cause that classroom setup has been a no-no with them for years. You know, you're up here looking down to me

and they had been in many of them, had enrolled in the public school in adult classes every year, and in about a month they start filtering out, you know, and the classes would close. They wouldn't have enough pupils to come, because they weren't reaching them as adults. They had the same kind of stuff and materials that I carried in there with me and something, like I say, it was something that hit me when talking, and I called them up individually to talk with them to see where they stood. (Thrasher and Wigginton Interview)

Robinson's literacy learning practices and values were embedded in the history she shared with the participants. In her interviews, she discusses how some of her choices of writing texts and learning materials were the result of that shared history and knowledge. Many of the participants' previous school experiences were negative. Robinson's history of being forced to learn how to do laundry when she aspired to learn music attached her to oppressive literacy experiences. Esau Jenkins's fourth-grade education resonated with humiliation and frustration at being forced to attend a school painted black. Other participants, including Anderson Mack, internalized the substantial barriers placed in the way of literacy access. But Bernice Robinson worked her shared history into her teacher–learner role, situating herself as part of the group while simultaneously maintaining the proper amount of space from the group necessary for instruction. In Citizenship Schools, participants forged an alliance against a common experience of oppressive learning while exemplifying the social nature of literacy.

We didn't have time to go through the printing ordeal, we don't have time to go through all the ceremony and stuff. You've got to work right on. I think one of the things I said that was sensitive and made them really just open up to me and be willing to learn was the fact that I said, "I'm not a teacher. We're here to learn together." And I think that just sort of set the stage for everything. Because this student–teacher thing is an "I'm up here, you're down there, and I'm going to teach you something." But by letting them know

that we're going to learn together; they were going to teach
me as much as I was going to teach them. I really did learn a
whole lot, believe me. (Thrasher and Wigginton Interview)

Entering the classroom as a member of the community removed
any special barriers between teacher and students.[9] We usually per-
ceive a move from being a member of the group to being a leader,
or from singing in the choir to becoming lead singer, as a matter of
distance. In Robinson's case, when she announces the fluidity of her
position as a member of the community, she clearly blurs the line
between the position of student and of learner.

Robinson capitalized on the idea of their shared history by encouraging learners to make their voices heard. This proved to be a
means of facilitating both learning and teaching. This move, the
natural result of Robinson's respect for participants as peers but
even more for her elders, was inspired by her belief that they had
more than enough knowledge to teach her what they wanted to
learn. This approach made it possible to calm any resistance participants might have had and allowed them to focus on literacy
acquisition.

"BUT THIS SPOT OF GROUND THAT THEY LEAVE ME": INTERCHANGEABLE ROLES AND NEW MEANINGS

Citizenship School participants operated from a tradition of weaving literacy practices and meanings together with personal autonomy, identity, and self-esteem.[10] While resisting dominant social forces, participants did critical intellectual work as they took
control of their teaching and learning. It's important to recognize
that this moves beyond common, limited civic-centered literacy
acquisition motives. Clearly, resistance takes place when participants *refuse* to focus their teaching and learning only on civic or
political material. Further, the dominant (white) social forces that
set the learning activities and materials of adult African American
learners at a juvenile level were met by resistance and an alternate
perspective, which included the assertion of individual and group
autonomy—i.e., participants decided what was important to learn
and why. Resistant response was a space in which participants

created deviations from the initial call by striving to individually and collectively shape their literacy learning. In other words, it was a place where the individual and the group resisted and/or changed preestablished social and political methods and motives. This principle—resistance to preconceived notions of their literacy focus or needs—provides a means of exploring the individual intellectual practices, meanings, and values of literacy learning. While individual participants expressed a unified interest in learning, they also resisted by taking control of teaching and learning ideologies, even if they came from inside the group. In the Citizenship School experience, call-and-response becomes analytical practice that requires the admission of diverse voices and diverse experiences. It's an ideology that supports an inclusive critique greater than any individual analysis (Werner, *Playing* xvii).

The most damaging and long-term consequence of American slavery was the systematic elimination of identity, the effects of which can still be seen in black American communities today. The most obvious identity conflict can be found in the various racially defining labels we adopted: Negro, Colored, Black, Afro-American, African American (with or without the hyphen). The ability to determine one's own identity is part of the quest for personal freedom.

Jenkins's and Sea Islands residents' response to the initial call for social justice activism affirmed the value of literacy for civic responsibility (voting), but the subsequent response changed the direction of the initial call, transforming the primary goals of literacy acquisition into the principles of empowerment and autonomy, self-esteem, identity, and freedom. This battle for literacy acquisition expressed a desire for freedom and self-determination that is deeply rooted in even contemporary black culture. Citizenship School participants' response to the initial call began with a collective made-up mind: a determination to seize freedom from Jim Crow segregationist policies. Adult African Americans who sought literacy understood the meanings of freedom. For most Citizenship School participants, freedom represented not only access to full citizenship rights but also a means by which to gain spatial autonomy, or freedom of movement.[11]

Anderson Mack Sr. was a participant who negotiated his Citizenship School participation not only to sustain his freedom but also to cultivate his role as an activist and community organizer. He credits the Citizenship Schools with helping him to become a community leader. During our long discussions, Mack explained that at the age of twenty-two, with only a second-grade education, he participated in the Wadmalaw Island Citizenship School. When the classes ended, Mack continued to attend adult classes at the Haut Gap High School on Johns Island. He ultimately used literacy to maintain employment and get promotions while working for the Charleston County Public Works Department, a job he kept for thirty years. As a result of his steady income, he was able to pay his property taxes, allowing him to maintain landownership. Control over his land greatly increased his autonomy.

The value of landownership, to Mack and other adult African Americans, is clear in his description of how he acquired his land. Recalling the mandate to never relinquish the family land, he details why he had to learn to write his name: "Then my grand[parents] die. They die when I was sixteen years old. But this spot of ground that they leave me which they order me to take care of. And I tell them I would work on the farm. And I keep everything they leave for me. They had cows. I keep." For Mack, freedom was situated within the value of owning land.

During the 1950s, the Sea Islands were starting to become recognized as valuable property for hotel and resort developers. Consequently, landowners faced increasing pressure to sell. Mack's freedom was jeopardized in 1955 when he was informed that as a landowner he was required to *sign* his name on the deed for his property—the customary *X* would no longer be acceptable. This change motivated his desire to learn to write—literacy meant maintaining his personal freedom. He realized it was crucial to learn to read and write if he was to keep his "ground." He told me that this land was such a valuable possession that he was committed to maintaining it for generations, ordering his own children never to sell it.

Economic sovereignty also motivated the response to the initial call. In her research on the social implications of the Citizenship Schools, Sandra Oldendorf argues that during the 1950s, "the economic situation was grim. Black farmers had to go through middlemen to sell their produce. Since many of the farmers were illiterate, they were often cheated" ("Highlander" 36). Though he speaks in less abstract terms, Mack emphasizes a sense of freedom that parallels historian Orlando Patterson's definition of *freedom* as "not being coerced or restrained by another person in doing something" and having "the conviction that one can do as one pleases" (3). Mack states that because of his personal freedom, he was able to grow and sell crops as he pleased:

> At the time when I start raisin' a family working on my farm I was making twenty dollars a week. We was growing vegetables: beans, corn, and potatoes. [Working for public safety,] I do roadwork. I work with them, they was paying 60 cents an hour and I still do my little farmin' and take my own stuff to market. . . . Going to market I make more money than I make the whole week [in public works] in just one day. One thing I'll never forget. We plant a 50-pound bag of beans and things were cheap and the market was good. I made $750 dollars on a 50-pound bag of beans in harvest. These are things that help us to be where we are today.

Mack held tight to the relationship between personal freedom and literacy, which allowed him to maintain his economic base. He confirms that the primary reason he was able to farm his own land as well as maintain employment was directly connected to his motives for participating in the Citizenship School.

Different learners prioritized different motives, which manifested in the benefits they received. For example, Mrs. Janie Owens of Johns Island wrote of her pride in the work she could do as a result of learning to read and write: "I learn so much by going to it [Citizenship School] learn me how to read and pronounce my spelling and how to crochet [until] I can make anything I want." The various values of freedom were passed down from generation to generation. For example, Laura Johnson wrote about how she and her children benefited from the Citizenship School: "I am a member of the adult school of Wadmalaw Island and a mother of 10 children before I became a member of the adult school. I was wishing an wanted to learn how to read and figure & sew, since I became a member of the adult school I can make my children's clothes and also read and figure much better." These adult learners clearly express their gratitude at being able to make decisions free from coercion and restraint.[12]

The second dimension of Patterson's definition of freedom is that it is *sovereignal*, defined as "the power to act as one pleases, regardless of the wishes of others, as distinct from personal freedom, which is the capacity to do as one pleases, *insofar as one can*" (3–4). Both nineteenth- and twentieth-century learners expressed their belief that learning to read and write would afford them the ultimate authority over themselves. The power to determine their destiny was directly linked to learning to read and write. William Andrews, in *To Tell a Free Story*, summarizes the connections between the value of literacy, strength of mind, and self-determination: "The acquisition of literacy, the power to read books and discover one's place in the scheme of things, is treated in many slave narratives as a matter equal in importance to the achievement of physical freedom" (13). It's no secret that captives gained mobility as a direct result of literacy acquisition; essentially, mobility stemmed from the ability to write (Cornelius 73).

Anderson Mack, Alice Wine, and Janie Owens, along with others who attended the schools, acknowledged that they equated the acquisition of literacy with freedom to govern their own lives. Specifically, Mack used the writing skills he acquired in the Citizenship School to protect his independence and the power he had as a result of owning land. This value of freedom resonated in both his personal and professional lives. Mack was employed with the Charleston County Public Works as a laborer doing roadwork. Then, because of the increased confidence and self-respect he gained from learning to write his name, he was promoted to "operate machines and then to an assistant operator." His appointment to a supervisory position increased Mack's independent power in the workplace. He later became involved in community work and, along with other Citizenship School participants, helped to establish a local community center that currently sponsors a senior citizens program. Mack also worked to get mail delivered on Wadmalaw Island. He believed the tutelage and encouragement he received from his Citizenship School teacher Ethel Grumble helped build his confidence while at the same time cultivating his belief that, aside from his God, he had absolute power over his own life.

Other Citizenship learners explicitly connected learning to read and write to the sovereignal freedom they gained. Janie Owens wrote in a letter supporting the continuation of the schools that "most of all it learn me how to read." She stressed the personal supremacy that learning to read and write gave her over her life and how it affected her by stating, "It meant so much to me." She repeats this statement several times in her letter to Horton, emphasizing her extreme gratitude for the "lessons" she learned.

Call-and-response is a process that acknowledges diverse voices and diverse experiences, including the meaning(s) of civic freedom, within participants' teaching and learning activities. As discussed, the initial call set voting (civic inclusion) as the primary motive for literacy acquisition, even though participants widened the scope of that call. Voting is central to the idea of civic freedom that resonates within the response. Civic freedom becomes the capacity of adult community members to participate in its governance. A person feels free, has a recognized place in the community, and is involved in the way it is governed. The existence of civic freedom implies a political community of some sort, with clearly defined rights and obligations for every citizen.

Acquiring civic freedom was an empty goal for enslaved African Americans, most of whom, like the Citizenship School participants, saw individual empowerment and physical autonomy as their primary goals. Literacy acquisition was also a communal possession, a political demonstration of resistance to oppression and of self-determination.[13]

Because civic freedom was the primary value within the initial call for teaching and learning, Septima Clark, Highlander's educational director, wrote in one of her Citizenship School funding proposals that "the Citizenship School is an adult school, for people who need to learn the basic skills and information which will help them in voter registration and voting."[14] She went on to explain that the schools would be open to "all people of a community who face problems related to first-class citizenship and who want to do something about it."[15]

Most Citizenship School participants linked literacy directly to civic freedom. They acknowledged and practiced the initial call; however, as discussed, they also added a different perspective by reprioritizing the most important practices, meanings, and values. Alice Wine, Esau Jenkins, and Anderson Mack each expressed gratitude at being able to participate in governing their communities. In a more direct response, Johns Island resident Solomon Brown wrote:

I wish to express my appreciation for the adult school on Edisto Island. It was a great benefit to my people and me. We are very much interested in what the School is doing and stands for. We learned much of what Democracy means that we did not know before. We had some to register and many who are going to register. We learned what many words meant and a better way of expressing yourself. We were inspired to help others toward first class citizenship.[16]

Mrs. C. L. Vanderhorst of Charleston Heights and others supported Brown's sentiment. Vanderhorst wrote, "I can read better I also registered and vote it help me to be a better citizen." Rosalee Washington stated, "I wish you [Myles Horton] were running for President. I would sure cast my ballot for you."[17] These declarations were motivated by the fact that African American people were disenfranchised, and voter registration was a significant though not defining element of the teaching and learning.

For Anderson Mack, civic freedom was only part of the response to literacy activism. He used his new-found freedom not only to register to vote but also to become an active and respected community leader. He helped start the first child care center on Wadmalaw Island and worked with others to create a community center. He explained to me with great pride that this project required him to assist in purchasing several acres of land for the community. Mr. Mack passed his passion for civic accountability to his son, who now directs a housing rehabilitation program called the Sea Islands Rural Missions Community Agency.

During my interview with Anderson Mack, he expressed how being unable to read and write affected his self-esteem. His struggles to learn as an adult were based on his initial struggles to attend school. These challenges were not directly connected to voting, although one could speculate that proper legislation might have produced adequate transportation or paved roads. Mack said that when he was a small boy he was not able to begin school until the age of twelve: "At that time they really didn't have no decent road to walk. We have a lot of rain in the low country. They had something like a wharf in the low areas where you could travel across." Mack was not tall enough to cross the swamp and walk the planks until age twelve. As if this late start wasn't a big enough hurdle to clear, Mack's father removed him from school for more than a year after he got into trouble arguing over pecans with a neighbor's daughter. Mack recalled how difficult learning to write was for him as an adult:

> And I just get blank. I got blank. My head got blank. I was out of school for about a year before they send me back. I just couldn't function. The brain couldn't function. I don't know what happened. It just wouldn't function. When I come to the [Citizenship School] I couldn't sign my name. That was the bad part about it.

Mack explained that even holding a pencil was something he had to learn all over again. Bernice Robinson supports this challenge, noting that her teaching practices included instruction in how to hold a pencil and how to apply the right amount of pressure (see also Oldendorf, "Highlander").

Mack understood that his association with the Citizenship School helped him in several ways. He became a community leader and an activist, recruiting participants for the Wadmalaw Island classes. For him, the first step was not reading the South Carolina Constitution but claiming control over his name: "A lot of people back at that time couldn't read. Plenty of people. But who had the pride in themselves to go to the [Citizenship School]. That really help 'cause that help me; they teach me how to write my name."

Mack's literacy values are clear in the emphasis he places on why and how he faced literacy learning. His motive to learn to read and write was not voter registration. In South Carolina, property owners could vote as long as their land was valued at $300 or more. And reading the South Carolina Constitution was reserved for those who did not own property, which included a large number of African American people, so voting was not a major issue for Mack. He accentuated his pride not only in learning "standard English" but also in learning to write his name, which for him transformed his written identity from an *X* to standard written letters. He described learning to write with pride, offering specific details: "What she [Ethel Grimball] do is spell my name on something first, then I could start to print it. You know, A-n-d-e-r-s-o-n. Then she come to my last name. M-a-c-k. Then she type it up for me. Then after I print it she take my hand and try to join it." From the identification and pronunciation of the letters in his name, he was able to decode other words. Mack also acknowledged that an important benefit of his instruction was learning how to use "proper English." For example, he was taught the difference between *he* and *she*. Before attending the school, he called everyone "he." For Mack, being able to make this distinction was a great source of pride.

For adult learners, reading and writing their names was a challenging initial step toward autonomy and identity—self-respect. In most cases, learning to write was an important and serious practice. However, Septima Clark wrote about several "humorous incidents" that challenged the schools' kinesthetic teaching method. Mr. Jones, a Citizenship School participant, was told to trace his name; after seeing it, he declared "sternly" that this was not his name. "He pointed to an *X* he had made. 'That's my name. I've been writing it like this all these years, and I don't mean to change it now!'" (Clark, *Echo* 154–55). Another adult learner believed that by not signing his name with an *X* he would be "in trouble with the government. I ain't going to change my name" (Oldendorf, "Highlander" 72).

Mack's personal advantages were about more than basic writing. This is clear in the emotion he expressed when describing the difficulty he had functioning in a world with restrictive codes. This was an era inundated with signage directing him to his "proper place." The ability to show deference to oppressive forces was imperative for African Americans during the Jim Crow era. Mack explained that it was important to be able to read something as common as a bathroom sign. He described not only the embarrassment but also the fear involved in walking in the wrong door:

> The embarrassing thing in my life. Where is the ladies' bathroom and where is the men's bathroom? I don't know which one was [which]. And that's embarrassing. I thank God I can read that. The door sign is there [but] you still have to go and ask someone which door to go in.

Making a similar mistake in a white establishment would have placed him in physical jeopardy. Some signs were just too difficult to read, such as "We serve colored carry out only" or "Colored seated in the rear"; simply being able to identify the words *colored* and *white* was not always sufficient. Contrary to popular belief, a black person's primary fear was not limited to drinking fountains. The signs that read "Colored not allowed" were difficult to recognize and presented the greatest challenge. To further complicate things, some signs were misspelled.[18] According to Mack, postings were not always easy to read, such as "Wadmalaw white residents only." In most cases, children were told at an early age what places they could enter in their own communities. Mack observed, however, that when traveling to other communities, physical survival depended on being able to read segregationist signage. It has been well documented that during the Jim Crow era, if a colored man entered the wrong space, he was guaranteed to be "taught a lesson." The most common punishment was a beating, but one also could become the guest of honor at an old-fashioned lynching.

In her autobiography, Septima Clark supports Mack's observations, emphasizing the value of literacy as a tool for building self-esteem. She writes about Alice Wine, Esau Jenkins's first student, who, as a result of learning to read and write, received a better paying job. According to Clark, "she [Alice Wine] gets much pleasure in being able to read during her leisure time. And one day she told me what a great satisfaction it was for her to be able to write a simple letter to her brother, with whom for many years she had been unable to correspond" (*Echo* 154). This confirms that the initial call, which focused on voter registration, was both affirmed by school participants and changed to include individual values. Clark continues:

> One will never be able, I maintain, to measure or even approximate the good that this work among the adult illiterates on this one island has accomplished. How can anybody estimate the worth of pride achieved, hope accomplished, faith affirmed, citizenship won? These are intangible things but real nevertheless, solid and inestimable value. (154)

Citizenship was included in the values of literacy, but even Clark places it last in a list of personal (spiritual) meanings. The primary goal for instruction—and learners recalled this—was that learning to read and write should open up a world to which the doors had been closed for a long time. Anderson Mack stressed that his learning connected him to self-respect, influencing his ability to function in the world around him. Like Jenkins, he saw the economic benefits:

> On my job I started at sixty cents per hour and though I didn't have any education. But there is one thing in life, self-respect yourself. Know how to treat people. You have to have an education. You have to have self-respect. You have to be willing to work. If you have the chance to make it you have to have self-respect.[19]

He connects his self-respect to his willingness to learn to write, which also helped him gain control of his economic life:

I work and I show you how things can happen. I started as a laborer on my job. And I was willing to work and self-respect [meaning he had respect for himself]. Moved me from a laborer to operate machine and to an assistant operator. I didn't have any education, but what I get at the adult school.

For Mack, learning to write led to his promotion to a supervisory position on his job. This was a clear source of pride for him and more evidence that, when changed by participants, the direction of the initial call could expand the value of learning to read and write. It is important to mention that there were also negative responses to the initial voting-centered call. Mack described how he testified about the ways in which his experiences delivered him from intellectual bondage, noting that witnessing was his tool for recruiting people to participate in the Citizenship School. The initial call or goal was firmly rooted in voter registration, and many participants agreed with this call, but not everyone recognized literacy as a means to effect social changes. In spite of the successes of the Highlander project, most people in Mack's community who could have benefited from the schools did not attend because, as they told him, they were happy with things the way they were. Some people were afraid of the potential consequences of participating in the literacy program, convinced there was no value in citizenship education and, more important, no value in pursuing their right to vote. Mack went so far as to say that most adults in his community had been "brainwashed."

4

"I've Got a Testimony": Bearing Witness to a Historical Case of African American Curriculum and Instructional Methods

> We would form a circle, each touching those next to us so [as] to physically express our spiritual closeness. We "testified," speaking on the day's or the week's experiences. We shared the pain of those experiences and received from the group affirmations of our existences as suffering beings. As we "lay down our burdens," we became lighter. As we testified and listened to others testify, we began to understand ourselves as communal beings, no longer the "individuals" that the slave system tried to make us. . . . We sang and moved until we were able to experience totally the spirit within us. We "got happy.". . . We became, again, a community.
>
> Donna Marimba Richards, *Let the Circle Be Unbroken*

ON AUGUST 6, 1961, SEPTIMA CLARK AND Bernice Robinson facilitated a teacher training discussion focused on how to set up a Citizenship School. Topics included when to hold classes, how to organize class schedules, and how to obtain and use materials. They seriously considered Sea Islands cultural traditions when planning class dates and times so that classes did not interfere with seasonal farmwork or various weekly church and lodge meetings.[1] Therefore, classes were scheduled Monday through Friday, never on Sunday, and during the off-season for planting—January through the end of February. Robinson based these decisions on her own experiences living on the islands. She understood the value of motivating the learning process and the importance of integrating participants' literacy material into a broader and more complicated lifestyle. In addition, Robinson did not limit her choice of literacy tools to voter registration. Her curriculum, both learning and teaching, extended beyond civic inclusion to actualizing the intersections between the Sea Islands way of life and spiritual existence.

Robinson introduced participants to the material, urging them to critically question the Jim Crow social system. The curriculum was designed primarily to communicate valuable knowledge (testifying) while addressing the learners' curiosity about the world, introducing them to texts relevant to their culture and history and facilitating the acquisition of basic, moderate, and advanced knowledge in five main areas: writing instruction, reading instruction, leadership development, nontraditional creative instructional growth, and intellectual and spiritual development through social and political knowledge.[2]

Clark, Myles Horton, and Esau Jenkins encouraged Robinson to teach the first sessions, but they did not provide a lesson plan, texts, or curriculum. Left on her own, Robinson committed to an inclusive curriculum, a pragmatic approach that utilized practical learning materials and methods. In the same way that bearing witness requires recognition of both community and individual experiences, Robinson's focus on reading and writing skills merges topics of intense interest shared amongst learners and teachers.[3]

Robinson's literacy narrative reveals an attitude about learning and teaching arising from her personal learning experiences, which were primarily negative. In direct contrast to her own experiences, she draws on the testifying practice to create a communal bond through her narration. Enacting a dramatic narration or testimony, she explains her struggle of being forced from the seventh through ninth grades to participate in a curriculum consisting of cooking, ironing, sewing, and laundry:

> So that's the control that the teachers had in those days. We had to learn how to do laundry, we had to learn how to wash, we had to learn how to iron. All that was when you started in the seventh grade and went from the seventh through the ninth grade: cooking, sewing, and laundry. You didn't

ask whether you had to take it, you took it. You had to take it. The girls had to take that. And, uh, I remember that the teacher had me to iron a white shirt over and over again.

And I had to wash that shirt every time I had to iron it. I had to wash it out first and then I had to iron it again. Starch it and iron it. And the reason why is because on the collar, I would get what they called "cat faces"—creases, and I couldn't get it straight and of course, we didn't have any electric iron, you know. We had the flat irons, see? It was heated, you know, on the charcoal thing and you had to wipe it off and I would smear it, and I would get it—oohh, I said I never wanted to see a white shirt again in my life. (Thrasher and Wigginton Interview)

Like most American women—white as well as African American—Robinson's "public" education was limited to training as a domestic worker. She was denied any instruction that might encourage her to think critically. Robinson's greatest desire was to study classical music, but she faced a lack of material that could have increased her enthusiasm about learning. This repressive pedagogy determined her choices when developing the Citizenship School curriculum. Her testimony offers clues about both her learning and her teaching values, which were shaped through absence rather than positive experience. Robinson's literacy narrative highlights not only her humanity but also how she found *redemption* and recovered from an oppressive learning environment by participating in an empowering teaching and learning experience. Thus, the Citizenship School curriculum included communicating valuable knowledge and connecting it to broader social systems, embracing not only the secular ideology of the Civil Rights Movement but also a wider, shared belief in a sacred, spiritual transformative power.

Bearing witness is a concept that requires sharing valuable knowledge about larger contexts; in this case, it permeated Citizenship School curriculum and instructional methods. Bernice Robinson enacted this practice in her 1980s interviews about the Citizenship Schools, providing both a context for and an example of how she wove testifying into literacy acquisition and use in the Citizenship School curriculum. Her account illustrates how she practiced the concept of bearing witness as an intellectual exercise to analyze Citizenship School participants' learning practices.

According to Bernice Robinson's various accounts, the initial Sea Islands Citizenship School curriculum was developed based on the participants' expressed requests. This was a challenging task because participants were diverse in their motives for acquiring literacy as well as their needs; their reading and writing abilities ranged from basic to moderate and advanced. Consequently, the requested materials had to represent this range. In spite of her lack of official teacher training, Robinson courageously developed a curriculum that acknowledged a diverse knowledge base and integrated the everyday experiences of the learner in a way that reflected the whole person. This approach helped participants to overcome previous academic struggles while motivating and empowering them through the use of a critically conscious curriculum linked to larger social and political systems (e.g., the black church and the Civil Rights Movement).

Responding to the burdens of South Carolina voting history, Robinson collected learning materials for a primary text called *My Reading Booklet*, which included intellectual exercises designed to empower participants while forging resistance against dominant oppressive forces. She refers to this process as "turning on a light."[4] For example, in the practice of making reading and writing acquisition applicable as well as empowering, Robinson put together a spelling vocabulary list ranging from terms encountered in everyday life to the language of the South Carolina Constitution.[5] Taped class sessions illuminate how words such as *tomato, cotton, register,* and *imprisonment* were more relevant to daily living than reading lessons with language centered on *cat, dog,* or *Dick and Jane.* When designing the curriculum, Robinson listened to and internalized testimonies about participants' learning practices and experiences.

Admittedly, learning to read and write was the first goal of many participants. But reading and writing lessons encompassed more than learning how to complete voter registration forms. For some, learning to write their names gave them a sense of power and pride, evoking the transformative power of *Nommo* (see discussion in Chapter 1). In an interview with me, Anderson Mack emphasized that writing his name was crucial to completing many forms such as property deeds and paychecks (see Chapter 3).[6]

MY READING BOOKLET

Robinson was unable to locate appropriate material or textbooks, so she designed workbooks exclusively from those she had used in the initial Johns Island session in 1957. The first edition of this workbook, titled *My Reading Booklet 1958–1959*, was approximately twenty pages and included topics such as Highlander's Official Statement of Policy, Explanations; South Carolina Voting Laws and Vocabulary; South Carolina's Political Parties; Taxes You Must Pay in Charleston County; and How to Obtain Social Security Benefits. Later, after returning from a recruiting trip for Highlander in California, Septima Clark got involved in designing the writing lessons. Robinson advocated for the inclusion of writing exercises with information on how to write letters to the editor of a newspaper and how to write names and addresses on a mail-order form. Participants placed a high value on how and what to write on a money order. Other exercises included directions on how to speak to public officials. Robinson and Clark also made sure the workbooks contained sample forms for writing practice.

From 1958 to 1959, Robinson taught using the first two editions of the workbook. From 1961 to 1962, the books were revised, and the title was changed to *My Citizenship Booklet*. This edition emphasized learning to read and write explicitly for the purpose of voter registration. The seventeen-page booklet begins by stating the purpose:

> The citizenship schools are for adults. *The immediate program is literacy.* It enables students to pass literacy tests for voting. But there is involved in the mechanics of learning to read and write an all-around education in community development which includes housing, recreation, health and improved home life. Specific subjects are emphasized [such]

as safe driving, social security, co-operatives, the income tax, and an understanding for tax supported resources such as water testing for wells and aid for handicapped children. The citizenship schools provide a service to the people which is not available through any other private or public programs at the present time. It is open to all people of a community who face problems related to first-class citizenship and want to do something about them.[7] (emphasis mine)

It is not clear who wrote this passage, but the booklet is a testimony to the value of literacy for participants. The booklet served as a means of resisting dominant forces that situated civic inclusion—voting—as central to learning. Making their individual and cultural literacy values the priority, participants exerted power and authority over the learning material.

The contents of the workbooks show how participants, both learners and teachers, endorsed and embraced a testifying epistemology as well as a collective respect for a critically conscious curriculum. When Robinson and Clark developed the curriculum, they may have anticipated that some learners would come to the material thinking like individuals, but they expected that those people would take what they learned from the material out into the community, raising critical questions by witnessing, which would in turn promote collective empowerment.[8]

The Citizenship School curriculum required learners not only to become aware of problems in their world and the world of others but also to begin asking questions about these problems as well as proposing solutions. At first glance, the workbook appears to contain basic exercises that encourage participants to take control of their reading and writing aptitude. A close analysis of Robinson's testimony on her development of the curriculum, as well as the material she chose, reveals how the exercises became a means of motivating participants to take pleasure in improving their knowledge, especially regarding their communities, the larger world, and their place in it. Typically, a critical consciousness curriculum requires an identification of the strengths and weakness of one's culture and of conflicts between what is and what should be (Ladson-Billings,

Dreamkeepers). In this context, critical consciousness is a process of becoming empowered through the acknowledgment of both sacred and secular forces, in addition to skepticism. Testifying requires a group experience, which is an emotionally dramatic exchange. It was common practice for participants who attempted to register to vote to share their voting successes and failures with the group, a mark of a gospel literacy testifying ideology. As a means of expanding literacy acquisition and use to the larger world, the curriculum included letter-writing exercises meant to initiate discussion about the power of letter-writing campaigns to local and national newspapers.

Further analysis illustrates how testifying principles intersect with a curriculum contextualized within the larger Civil Rights Movement. The second edition of *The Citizenship Booklet* (1959–1960) includes a reading and writing exercise titled "Our America"; this passage is excluded from booklets after 1961. The page includes an outlined map of South Carolina sketched over an outline of the United States. The map shows where Charleston and the Sea Islands are located in relation to the rest of the country. On the surface, the map and passage appear to be a simple geography or reading and writing lesson. But the passage under the picture reads as follows:

> This is a map of the United States of America. It is the home of a great American Nation. We are a part of that great nation. We are all Americans. Our home is on islands in the Atlantic Ocean in Charleston County on the southeast coast of South Carolina. We love this great land. It has given us our children and grandchildren. Day by day we silently pour the concrete of love into the furious violent ocean of hate. Some day that concrete will build a foundation that will support a bridge to span the channel and open lines of communication to all peoples. Our hearts are filled with that spirit of brotherhood and our hands move forward defying all acts of violence. The Supreme court building and its justices are the symbol of law. The White House is a symbol of the free representative government. We accept the results of election and abide by the

ruling of the courts. We in America know that an educated child is more important to the future than any other man's political future. The voice of the school child can be heard asking "What about me?" The American way is law and justice. Yes, we love this great land—American.[9]

Robinson's purpose for this exercise was to guide participant literacy practices toward voter registration. But that is a limited perspective; this passage indicates a different trajectory from that of the primary reading and writing material used in subsequent Freedom School books. In addition to being an intellectual exercise that shares valuable knowledge about the larger social context—America—it illustrates how literacy exercises promote spiritual practices by suggesting to the learner a sense of being part of something bigger than him- or herself, of being connected to something other than one's individual concerns. The passage is both a reading and writing exercise and a description of how American democracy works. With passages such as "We love this great land" and "It has given us our children and grandchildren," this curriculum integrates complex social, political, and spiritual concepts. Reading and writing exercises intersect with emotional feelings—"Our hearts are filled with that spirit"—about what it means to be an "American." This is an example of a curriculum developed in response to a problem—disenfranchisement—as well as a testimony that actualizes the unity between spiritual and material aspects of existence.[10]

Citizenship School participants engaged in individual acts of reading and writing equal to, and informed by, those undertaken in political and social systems. Participation included leadership development activities; therefore, the curriculum incorporated lessons on African American history and culture, organizational skills, and leadership ability. Robinson and Clark designed a curriculum centered on public speaking while also improving other communication skills.[11] Robinson knew that communication or speech classes were particularly crucial because, during the voting exam, if any word was pronounced incorrectly, people would not be allowed to register.[12]

In 1963, after the Southern Christian Leadership Conference (SCLC) took control of the Citizenship School program, Robinson and Jenkins developed a program they called "Second Step Political Education Classes."[13] This program stretched writing concepts beyond those of the initial and "official" Citizenship School classes. An analysis of the Second Step classes provides answers to questions about the type of political literacy learning that took place in the nontraditional curriculum. The purpose of the Second Step classes was to inform participants, through shared experiences including testimonies, what voting meant and how taking part could improve oppressive situations. In a recorded teacher training session, Robinson explained that "the goal of these [Second Step] classes was to create awareness for the political structure in the local community and across the state."[14] She emphasized that Second Step participants needed to understand who controlled the political power and funds and also who had important information and how individuals could qualify to run for public office. The Second Step classes rounded out the basic Citizenship School curriculum by joining nontraditional academic tools with political reading and writing exercises. For example, Robinson researched participants' learning requests and subsequently included in the curriculum subjects such as how to drive a car and get a driver's license. This aligns with Anderson Mack's assertion that before the Citizenship Schools opened many islanders drove "illegally and rather dangerously." Robinson's curriculum also included learning how to apply for Social Security benefits, how to file an income tax return, and how to open a checking account.

Second Step classes also included discussions on shared contemporary issues, encouraging participants to think critically about local situations in the context of national problems, and to view current issues in a more sophisticated way. Through class discussions, films, and speeches, participants learned that people in other parts of the country and world had similar problems and how they were working together toward social justice in their communities. While participants discussed global problems, they also learned how to access local resources. Participants began to identify strengths and weaknesses within Sea Islands culture as well as contradictions and conflicts between what is and what ought to be.

INTERSECTIONS: LEARNING
AND INSTRUCTIONAL METHODS

The initial Citizenship Schools were held on Johns Island in the winter of 1957. As word caught on, other islands were soon holding classes. According to Robinson, participants on Johns Island influenced others to participate through personal testimonies (i.e., giving a verbal account). Consequently, residents requested Citizenship classes in their communities. With the exception of Bernice Robinson, who was from Charleston, most of the appointed instructors were members of the Sea Islands community, including Aileen Brewer and Ethel Grimball.[15]

Ethel Grimball, Esau Jenkins's daughter, taught classes on Wadmalaw Island. In 1955, before taking on the responsibility of teaching Citizenship classes, Grimball had been promised a teaching job at Haut Gap High School on Johns Island, but shortly before the school year started, she was informed she no longer had a job. The school supervisor told Jenkins that the principal did not want any of Jenkins's children working in the district because of his work with the NAACP. Grimball took a job teaching science in Beaufort, another county away. She quit after a year and a half because she didn't want to travel so far from her home.[16] Unlike Robinson, Grimball was a college-educated teacher, but she too had close ties to the people on Johns and Wadmalaw Islands. Like other teachers, Grimball developed her own teaching methods, explaining that while she used materials designed for elementary school students, she used them in such a way that learners responded well to them (Oldendorf, "Highlander" 76). When I asked Anderson Mack for his impression of the teachers, he explained that the elementary material made little difference to him because in this situation his motivation to learn took precedence over the material. He added that Ethel Grimball was a "good teacher" and her method of instruction, which accompanied a respectful attitude immersed in the spiritual principles of courage, willingness, and patience, made the difference. I asked Mr. Mack about his overall experience with the school, specifically his initial writing instruction. His testimony, in which he lists step by step the physical act of learning to write, suggests that instruction was rote and mechanical. But the core of his testimony was imbued with pride and conviction:

> Well, what happen, this was a group of adult mens and ladies. I don't meet Miss Septima Clark. I think she was the head of the program. And Bernice Robinson work along with she [Ethel Grimball]. And. But the class was good. Really helpful. She [Grimball] help a lot of people. What she do [with me] is she spell my name on something first, then I could start to print it. Just like you got you letters on your shirt. You know, like M-I-L. [*during the interview I was wearing a UW–Milwaukee sweatshirt*] She spell my name. My name is A-N-D-E-R-S-O-N. Then when it come to "Mack" she type that up for me: M-A-C-K. Then after that I print it; then she took my hand and try to join it. That's what she do. And that give me a chance where I could join my name. I do practice a lot on it. I still practice.

Because she was a formally trained teacher and used primary school materials, Grimball approached teaching from a different place than Robinson. However, through Mack's testimony, we see how a witnessing ideology permeates Grimball's instructional methods. Instead of *telling* Mack *how* to write, she demonstrates how a shared call for a fundamental unity gets actualized through literacy acquisition and use. Mack also explained to me that Grimball helped a lot of people through her testimony.

In the winter of 1958, a Citizenship class was started on Edisto Island and taught by Aileen Brewer. Brewer was a social worker from the local Presbyterian Church, which in turn furnished a meeting place. This was larger than the one on Wadmalaw, enrolling thirty-eight people, the largest class to that point. Like Robinson and Grimball, Brewer used instructional methods that included grouping students so that they could help one another. Also like Robinson and Grimball, Brewer responded to participants' needs by teaching reading, writing, arithmetic, citizenship, sewing, and leather craft. They all taught US history and used newspaper articles to discuss the Civil Rights Movement. Grimball incorporated visual aids such as maps and a globe (Brewer, "Final Report"). Teachers in the Citizenship Schools came from within the community. They were retired schoolteachers, ministers, housewives, and unemployed workers. Highlander Folk School staff believed that teachers from the community would have a better understanding of the culture, language, and lifestyle of its residents; they could understand and share experiences and the burdens of everyday life. Citizenship School teachers were people the learners could identify with. Clark and Horton believed that the best teachers were those with little or no formal training and that "they make better teachers than persons with a great deal of academic background" (Clark, *Echo* 46). This is not to say that professional teachers did not volunteer to teach; they did. But the greatest efforts went toward recruiting and training local community people to be teachers. Citizenship Schools required that teachers:

1. Be at least 21 years of age with some high school education or a college student,
2. Be able to read well aloud,
3. Be able to write legibly on the blackboard,
4. Be from the local community, and
5. Know or find out the location of the voter registration offices, name of officials, local available health care facilities, and the location of the social security office. (Highlander Folk School, n.d.)

Robinson recruited teachers the same way she sought out participants: all were identified through the church and by recommendations from local African American leaders. During the 1964 Freedom Summer, college students from all over the country volunteered to work as teachers. When the SCLC took over the Citizenship School program in 1962, they based teacher training on the Highlander Folk School model initiated with the Sea Islands Citizenship Schools. Teacher training varied from one to three weeks depending on the sponsoring organization. The workshops were based around the following ideas: learning and purpose go hand in hand, teachers should be made to feel a part of something significant by working together for a purpose, and the larger context is always discussed along with how to gain political power and make a better life for the community, state, nation, and world (Horton and Freire 67).

The teacher training programs were offered to people who were interested in organizing a Citizenship School in their local community. The workshops were held around the clock, Sunday through Friday. The curriculum included an orientation evening, which resembled Smitherman's example of a testifying service: "a ritualized form of black communication in which the speaker gives verbal witness to the efficacy, truth and power of some experience in which all blacks have shared" (Smitherman, *Talkin' and Testifyin'* 58). Each participant introduced him- or herself while communicating valuable knowledge as well as life experiences, relating them to larger social systems. This was followed by a day of demonstration classes, which focused on methods of teaching reading and writing. Participants were asked to observe, criticize, and, as learners, act as teachers. Aimee Horton, daughter of Myles Horton, describes the training sessions as follows:

> The students [prospective teachers] were asked to participate in the process, through demonstration classes, role-playing, and small group sessions where they formulate their own plans and educational programs. . . . This learning activity indicates that it "gives the students the experience of taking out some of his ideas," affords him the "benefit of the group's reaction" and "produces in the student the feeling of having made a commitment" . . . for themselves and to demonstrate activities which . . . would be included in the local Citizenship Schools. The singing, with a professional song leader, would include Negro folk and religious songs which was suggested their students would enjoy and at the same time, increase their reading vocabularies. (qtd. in Gyant 98)

Participants were not professional teachers, so every lesson was an example of good teaching (Cotton 4).[17] In other words, every session included a testimony that demonstrated to the participants what good teaching was about. To create a safe, comfortable environment, teachers were encouraged not to tell information but to ask for participation. Most important, teachers were asked to create ways to communicate their valuable life experiences through their development of instructional material. For example, teachers improvised verses of sacred and secular songs with verses based on their own experiences. During the training sessions, they learned how to use government pamphlets as a tool for discussion; newspaper articles could demonstrate biases and teach critical reading and writing. By the end of the teacher training workshop, participants learned how to organize and facilitate Citizenship classes.

The outline for the teacher training program illustrates that reading and writing instruction for both teachers and learners included vocabulary, story writing, filling out forms, writing letters, and writing arithmetic problems. In addition to addressing the words that made up the list of criminal offenses on the voter registration application, the vocabulary lessons show how teaching was contextualized within the Civil Rights Movement. For example, participants studied the meanings and gained command over words such as *dollar, attorney, sheriff, sit-in, magistrate, imprisonment, power, rebellion*, and *register*. These words were all central to articles being written during this era. Even more important, knowing who the sheriff was and exactly the reach of his jurisdiction proved helpful during many Civil Rights protests.

Citizenship School writing exercises included the call-and-response model described in the previous chapter. In this context, teaching writing as well as learning to write was a means of keeping everyday social and political issues up front, thus investing in individual and communal critical consciousness. For instance, the narratives participants learned to write and recite contained witnessing concepts that helped communicate valuable knowledge such as exactly how far it was to Atlanta, Charlotte, or Montgomery, and exercises to teach methods of mass participation. This included making meaning from life experiences such as the increase in civic power—counting registered voters. Whenever possible, teaching and learning were explicitly related to larger social systems. In the following example, math story problems include questions about growing and selling vegetables, activities most islanders engaged in. Here we see how the Citizenship School curriculum was used to promote activism:

> If you made three automobile trips to Atlanta and it is 735 miles round-trip, how many miles have you traveled? _____
>
> Henry will need _____ feet of wire to enclose a garden 6 yd. long and 8 yd. wide.
> The Crusader for Voters sent 187 people to register in January, 210 people in February, and 422 people in March. How many people were registered in three months? (*My Citizenship Booklet* 1961–1962)

The arithmetic problems not only fostered academic development but also motivated participants to think critically about economic development while encouraging them to think about what it would take to make a trip in order to participate in the larger Civil Rights Movement. They could think about trips to places like Atlanta, which during this time was a site of political activism. Like testifying, the curriculum provided a means to report on or share a triumphant experience. At times these were visual accounts of prophetic incidents such as Mr. Mack's experience with the profit he made from his garden. He explained to me with extreme affirmation: "One thing I'll never forget. We plant a 50-pound bag of beans and things were cheap and the market was good. I made $750 dollars on a 50-pound bag of beans in harvest." However, because the class collectively shared experiences raised through the curriculum, individuals were also able to share spiritual accounts that included feelings of faith, hope, courage, and perseverance. As part of the larger community, participants discussed specific oppressive, racist practices. Teachers learned to use the creative curriculum and instructional methods to testify and encourage one another to take action against Jim Crowism. In some of the class sessions, these creative instructional methods included oral exercises. A tape recorder was often employed to encourage participants to testify on everyday experiences. At the same time, the recorder was a tool for practicing diction and public speaking. This provided an opportunity for vocabulary and sentence development. Writing from dictation developed listening skills, writing persuasive material helped participants with intellectual development, and filling out application and voter registration forms and money orders was part of every writing exercise. Robinson explained that as a teacher she participated in the writing exercises, learning how to write summaries of their discussions.

Reading activities involved reading newspapers, magazines, and stories for comprehension, as well as the introduction and evaluation of new words, which involved use of a dictionary. Other instructional activities included drawing and role playing, interpreting tables, homework, and testing. Rather than teaching these activities separately, teachers allowed each one to flow into the other, and materials were developed from situations and experiences familiar to participants. These activities, along with the Citizenship Schools' four basic curriculum and instructional areas—writing and reading instruction, leadership development, intellectual development of social as well as political knowledge, and nontraditional creative instructional development—reinforced the relationship between the acquisition of knowledge and everyday life.

Just as with learners, a witnessing epistemology permeated the teachers' attitudes toward making meaning. By virtue of their participation in Citizenship School workshops, teachers had more than self-centered individual concerns. Here is where Paulo Freire's pedagogical theory from *Pedagogy of the Oppressed* is helpful, at least in thinking of the teacher less as one who must deposit knowledge and be omniscient and more as another learner. The teacher may know a little more about a topic or context, but culturally and critically conscious teachers see themselves as *facilitators* of knowledge. Teachers are learners too when they understand that they are learning from the students as well as along with their students. While they might know a little more about reading or the skill of writing, they relearn what it means to be a writer and a reader from each individual student. This is especially true in the case of the literacy teaching and learning practices of the Citizenship School teachers. Most of the teacher testimonies, in particular those by Bernice Robinson, endorse this philosophy. In almost every interview, speech, and recorded testimony, Robinson reiterates her declaration of the first night of class—"I'm not a teacher, we're here to learn together,"—reflecting, above all, her desire to closely connect with the class. Illustrating witnessing principles, Robinson affirms her humanity, negating the potential isolation of the teacher. The group reaffirms her when she announces her willingness to learn along with the community. She considered herself a member of the group, and in most of her narratives she hesitates to refer to participants as students. Instead, when she talks about them she uses their given names, and during instructional sessions or when reflecting back, she calls them "people," not students.

The acts of reading and writing mean different things to different people. From the requested material and the written responses of Citizenship School participants, it's clear there was diversity in the ways participants used their acquired knowledge. At this step, the teacher was not the expert; she or he primarily helped participants find their threshold into literacy. An interesting metaphor used by an unidentified teacher during a teacher training workshop summarizes this philosophy as follows: "I tell people, I'm not Jesus Christ. I didn't die on the cross for you. I cannot carry you over to Canaan. You have to walk over there for yourself."[18] In essence, the teachers saw learning as the student's choice to get to the "Promised Land." Teachers would play the role of Moses as long as they needed to, but ultimately salvation or redemption was up to the learner.[19] In other words, students determined the threshold and the mandate (Royster, *Traces* 275) of their own learning. Teachers had some say, but ultimately, the participants learned what they wanted to learn. The teachers merely facilitated the process.

By intersecting her life experiences with the Citizenship curriculum, Bernice Robinson developed nontraditional instructional methods. Her whole language approach predated and prefigured the widespread adoption of whole language literacy instruction in the 1970s and 1980s, a space in which her creative intellectual development might well have been officially legitimized. She explains her instructional process as follows:

> I started off with things that were familiar with them. They were working in the fields and I'd have them tell me stories about what they did out in the fields and what they had in their homes. I'd write these stories out and work with them on the words. I'd say now, "This is your story. We're going to learn how to read your story." (Oldendorf Interview)

If we extend the whole language philosophy to include concepts of witnessing, Citizenship School literacy activities illustrate a unity between spiritual and material aspects of participants' existence.

Robinson's teaching methods included reading and writing with students (the participant observer role), viewing the teacher as a learner, individual instruction, and having students author their own writing and reading exercises. When asked about her instructional methods, Robinson began by explaining how she taught writing:

> Naturally, everybody wanted to learn how to write their name. I never used printing. Because from my own experience that being an adult, I don't print anything. . . . If you fill out an application they'll say print your name up top, but you gotta sign it on the bottom. And adults have to sign their names to everything. . . . I knew that they had to sign their names, so we started with cursive writing so that they would learn how. . . . I used poster board to put their names on and have them trace over the writing. (qtd. in Gyant 94)

Because the schools had neither formal instruction materials nor photocopying machines, supplies for classes were mimeographed manually or hand-copied. During the first Citizenship School sessions, Robinson traced money orders onto fourteen pieces of cardboard so that all the participants could practice filling them out. She brought in supermarket ads for math lessons and wrote vocabulary words from voter registration applications on the chalkboard.

She had the eight participants who could not write at all trace their signatures over pieces of cardboard. Practicing the concept of testifying, learners told stories about their daily activities, which were then read aloud by participants who had moderate to advanced writing and reading proficiency.

Robinson's descriptions of the instructional sessions illustrate her learning process as well as how she developed an inclusive classroom. Her accounts also demonstrate that she considered intellectual development to be a complex notion that was not amenable to a single static measurement. In the following report to Clark, Robinson recounts how she used the curriculum to develop participants' social and political knowledge:

> The school which we planned for three months is in progress and the people have shown great interest. They are so anxious to learn. I have fourteen adults, four men and ten women, and there are thirteen high school girls enrolled to learn sewing. There are three adults that have had to start from scratch because they could not read or write. I start out with having them spell their names. About eight of them can read a little, but very poorly. So far I have been using that part of the South Carolina Constitution that they must know in order to register. From there, I take words that they find hard to pronounce and drill them in spelling and pronunciation and also have the meaning of the words so they will know what they are saying. We have to give them some arithmetic. The men are particularly interested in figures. I have never before in my life seen such anxious people. They really want to learn and are so proud of the little gains they have made so far. When I get to the club [Progressive Club] each night, half of them are already there and have their homework ready for me to see. I tacked up the Declaration of Human Rights on the wall and told them I wanted each of them to be able to read and understand the entire thing before the end of the school.[20]

Using the United Nations' Universal Declaration of Human Rights as a tool to teach reading and writing was a way to expose participants to new ideas with which they could evaluate their own world.

Robinson put this document on the wall, using it to teach vocabulary while asking participants to understand its meaning before the end of the three-month class. The universal human rights claimed in the declaration included freedom from discrimination based on race, color, sex, language, religion, politics, national social origin, birth, or other status; the right to life, liberty, and security; equal protection before the law; freedom from inhumane treatment or punishment; presumption of innocence; freedom of religion, expression, assembly, speech, and press; the right to take part in government; and the right to an education. These rights are considered essential in a document the United States supported for the rest of the world; through critical analysis, making meaning, and sharing communal experiences, Citizenship School participants could provide plenty of evidence that these rights were nonexistent for many poor people and minorities in the United States itself. Citizenship School participants joined literacy acquisition and use to the fundamental concepts of democracy. One participant's letter indicates how they used principles of testifying to become empowered over the burden of oppression through the development of social and political knowledge:

> I wish to express my appreciation for the adult school on Edisto Island. It was a great benefit to me and my people. We are very much interested in what the School is doing and stands for. We learned much of what Democracy means that we did not know before. We had some to register and many who are going to register. We learned what many words meant and the better way of expressing yourself. We were inspired to help others toward first class citizenship.[21]

Intellectual development included efforts to increase critical consciousness. Therefore, the curriculum included reading local and national newspapers and magazines such as the *New York Times* and the *Charleston Gazette*. Exercises helped participants to be more critical about what they read in the newspapers and the promises made to them by people who wanted their support. Robinson taught lessons on how to "read between the lines" by discussing with learners what newspaper articles really meant or what was left out. She guided participants through exercises that helped them question and differentiate between articles written locally and those from United Press International and the Associated Press. One assignment consisted of bringing in articles along with questions about them.

The teachers also responded to participants' other material interests, such as crafts and sewing. Many participants wanted these skills in order to better provide for their families or to obtain a marketable skill. Bernice Robinson was herself a seamstress and offered sewing as part of the early Citizenship curriculum. Although the crafts and sewing were not emphasized in the initial call for literacy learning, they were a valuable asset to many of the learners and may have motivated some of them to come to class. In a report on the progress of the Citizenship Schools, Esau Jenkins testified about how instruction went beyond basic literacy instruction to address the intellectual development of social and political knowledge:

> They not only teach them how to read and write, but they teach them how to do other things. They see the pictures (movies) of the walk to freedom and a lot of people enjoy seeing that. And all the pictures are very educational. And we talk about how you go about taking part in civic and government and voting making you better people. All these things we discuss in that school and a lot [of] people, some of them didn't know how to do it. Even fixin' money orders, they didn't know how to do it. Bernice Robinson teach them how to do that and I teach them how to be better people. How to conduct [yourself] in public. Check they insurance. Know when your books are paid up and all those things.[22]

Although the instructional methods of the early Citizenship School teachers varied, basic attitudes reflected similar literacy learning values. All teachers respected the participants as adults. All based the classes on what participants valued as meaningful knowledge for practical use. All took great pleasure in participants' accomplishments, no matter the level. All saw the need to challenge participants with the idea that literacy acquisition and use was their individual responsibility. And all saw learning to read and write as a necessary path to accessing the world. At the graduation ceremony for the first Citizenship class on February 6, 1957, Bernice Robinson stated:

> READ!! Read everything you see even if you don't understand what you're reading; read it anyway. Because that is the only way you are going to improve, is by practicing. Practicing becomes a habit and once you acquire a habit you will always do it. So I want you to keep at your work, though you're not in school; just pretend that you are coming and preparing yourself so that when the school reopens again, so that you will be way ahead of the rest.[23]

Although Robinson based her teaching on participants' academic levels, she also emphasized the intersections of everyday life with what they learned to read and write. Encouraging the first class to participate in their communities, Robinson again invoked the spiritual consciousness of being connected to something bigger than oneself:

> Now we have a little token here for you from Highlander School. I tried to get Ms. Clark to give this to you because I feel she represents Highlander. And it's coming through Highlander. But she insists that since I've been your teacher, that I should award you these little certificates. I hope that you will feel as proud of this little paper as I am to give it to you. It shows that you have attempted to reach out and into the world and see the other side. And get a little light into your life. You know we can never, never acquire too much knowledge. There is always something to be learned. And every time you learn something new there is another little light that has been entered into your life. And if I have brought just a little shaft of light into the lives of any of you here tonight, I feel good about it. As I call your name, I want you to come forward and receive your little certificate of award.[24]

Robinson knew that an important part of helping people become participants in their own learning was for them to identify their individual problems.[25] Robinson's "light" metaphor refers to a traditional freedom song, "This Little Light of Mine." It was adapted by Robinson and the Citizenship Schools as representative of the multirhythmic curriculum and instructional activities.

In 1959, music became a regular part of the curriculum and instructional activities.[26] This was possible largely through the work of Guy Carawan, who became Highlander's music director in 1959 after the death of Zilphia Horton. The Carawans explained to me that they moved to the Sea Islands and lived among the people in the late 1950s. Before Guy Carawan's arrival, music was not a central part of the curriculum. From 1959 on, however, Carawan participated in many of the Citizenship Schools' reading and writing sessions. Although he wrote out the lyrics to many of the traditional Sea Islands songs, participants also used writing as a way to learn the songs. For instance, he and Robinson developed a creative traditional activity that required adapting the lyrics to traditional Sea Islands songs such as "Michael, Row the Boat Ashore," a tune that originated on the Sea Islands in the 1850s.[27] Carawan would bring the written lyrics to class and participants would read along as they sane their special version of the song.

Carawan encouraged participants to tell their stories and share their individual music selections. In an effort to preserve Sea Islands culture, as discussed in Chapter 1, Guy and Candie published a book titled *Ain't You Got a Right to the Tree of Life?* The "tree of life," in the gospel spiritual from which the phrase is taken, symbolizes heaven. But the message, like gospel music concepts, was that the fruit from the tree of life should be enjoyed in *this* life and benefit the people on the Sea Islands. The Carawans' book not only documents the testimonies of many Sea Islands residents from the early to mid-twentieth century, it also illustrates how Sea Islands residents combined intellectual with spiritual growth. Myles Horton supported the use of gospel spirituals to teach reading and writing, reporting that in addition to social and political action, "'people need something to cultivate the spirit and the soul'" (qtd. in Old-endorf, "Highlander" 79). Assigning old island folk songs and new songs of the Civil Rights Movement was perceived as a means of adding an important ingredient to building the motivation and group consciousness necessary to boost self-confidence.

One primary reason for the success of the teachers was that they respected the Sea Islands culture. A significant part of this culture was music: music was a big part of African American churches on the South Carolina Sea Islands, and it became a part of the Citizen-ship Schools. Including Sea Islands music in the curriculum facili-tated the move toward empowerment. The next step was to guide participants from what they already knew to ideas that were new to them. Robinson, Ethel Grimball, and Aileen Brewer sought to open up new worlds to participants. Aileen Brewer wanted par-ticipants to be aware not only of their own world but also of the struggles of people elsewhere in the world.

CLASSROOM-IN-ACTION

Citizenship School instructors incorporated basic disciplinary content into their curriculum—math, reading, writing, and so-cial studies. However, learning events included discussions about sociopolitical issues. These discussions could turn into serious de-bates depending on the level of critical consciousness, responsive-ness, and energy the participants determined the topic warranted. In this section, I analyze an actual class-in-action, illustrating how everything is working together—witnessing, curriculum, teachers, and learners. I particularly focus on a discussion that shows how a simple demonstration on completing a voter registration appli-cation—which primarily meant checking boxes and writing short phrases, dates, and addresses—became a means of testifying and sharing ways of knowing. This particular lesson turned into a de-bate over concerns about how individuals understood the idea of freedom. During this lesson, participants responded to a dilemma of interpretation, gaining power over language saturated with op-pressive meanings. The following dialogue is from actual class-room exchanges and documents how participants processed ways of knowing, expanding their literacy learning through testimony. Participants embrace their power and autonomy over language (literacy) knowledge, acquisition, and use.

Because the instructional goal was for teachers and learners to move along a parallel plane, teachers were willing to let students determine their own destinations. This philosophy of literacy is clear through an analysis of the intellectual spaces in which instruction was taking place. On January 7, 1960, Aileen Brewer, the Edisto Island Citizenship School teacher, instructs participants on how to complete a voter registration application. She begins the lesson by calling out to participants like a gospel soloist inviting the choir to join in. She tells the participants exactly what to write on each line. They repeat her call. She then uses the chalkboard for instrumental accompaniment while simultaneously practicing exactly how certain information should look. Participants repeat the word or phrase she has written and, as if they have rehearsed to perform in unison, they repeat the call. The exchange goes as follows:

> BREWER: All right, now let's look at the other part so that we can get through. This is to certify that . . . and you will write your name on the next line. Write your name. Write your name.
> BREWER: . . . [*a questioning statement*] Is the register elector of what county? What county do you live in? Charleston County.
> GROUP RESPONSE: Charleston County.
> BREWER: [*repeats*] Charleston County. . . . Street? In the city or town of? You would put town of what? Edisto. Edisto Island.
> GROUP GESPONSE: Edisto Island

This exchange continues for about ten to fifteen minutes. The emphasis stays on filling in the necessary information needed to apply for a voter registration certificate. But because Brewer knows the content, stating that she has studied South Carolina's voting laws, she is able to testify—sharing her registration experience—to participants about alternate ways of qualifying to vote. Her account includes informing residents that by owning $300 worth of property, they need only to prove they pay property taxes. While this question is on the application, it is not clear whether this qualifies a person to forgo the literacy test before voting. I asked Anderson Mack to explain his perspective on this ambiguity. Voter registration was optional, he said; learning to write his name to hold on to his land was not:

> See, what happened, see like I tell you, we owned this property. And you paid a certain amount of taxes. See, if you couldn't read [but] you paid a certain amount of taxes you still could vote. In the time before my time our pastor told me that they threatened their life if they could read. They had to read the constitution whether they had property or not. But coming down the line, they make it easier. You had so many people couldn't read and since they make it easier if you pay your tax. I never did read. The truth is the light.

Mack supports the claims about property while demonstrating the testifying concept. He gives a verbal account about the truth and power of a tradition of oppressed literacy learning.

Brewer, however, acknowledges the uncertainty of Jim Crow's oppressive ideology, which included the registration process, and continued to encourage students to learn how to read and write sections of the South Carolina Constitution:

> BREWER: And number 4. [*reads*] I will demonstrate to the Registration Board that I can both read and write sections of the constitution of South Carolina; or "b," I own and have paid all taxes due at least, should be last year. On property in this state assessed at $300 or more? . . . Now if, umm. We hope that when you finish here you will be able to read or write some sections of the constitution. We also want help with that. We were wondering about that. We didn't know. We do have a copy of the constitution that we will—I mean all of us need to read some of

it. It's been very scarce and hard to get a hold of.

BREWER: The next is, if you are not able to read and write then you can show your certificate or your tax receipt that you have paid taxes on at least $300 dollars' worth of property. Not that you have paid $300 in tax, but that the value of the property is $300.

PARTICIPANT: If you have the tax receipt at home you will be able to register?

BREWER: $300 worth of property. Any property personal or real, I understand: plows, Frigidaires, and, umm, electrical appliances would be considered as personal property. Or we could have a tax receipt that we are paying taxes on real estate: real property, which would be houses and land and so forth.[28]

Knowing the curriculum, the participants' culture, and how to teach the content helps Brewer get through this section of the application. As the following exchange demonstrates, however, participants were not willing to let what they considered critical concepts pass without intense intellectual discussion. They were in a learning space that valued the intellectual development of social and political knowledge; they were free to ask questions about the form's language in an effort to gain or demand clarity. The participants refused to simply move on without it. The voter registration application required a prospective South Carolina voter to pledge that he or she was not guilty of an interesting list of offenses. These words were also included in the vocabulary reading and writing lessons. It reads as follows:

I have never been convicted of any of the following crimes: burglary, arson, obtaining goods or money under false pretenses, perjury, forgery, robbery, bribery, adultery, bigamy, wife beating, housebreaking, receiving stolen goods, breach of trust with fraudulent intent, fornication, sodomy, incest, assault with intent to ravish, miscegenation, larceny, or crimes against the election laws; or have been legally pardoned for such conviction. (*My Reading Booklet 1958–1959* 4–5)

Citizenship School pedagogy had a wider meaning beyond the classroom because it explicitly sought to socially construct shared experiences. This confirms Ladson-Billing's theory that culturally relevant teaching and learning "will organize and disorganize a variety of understandings of our natural and social world in particular ways" (*Dreamkeepers* 14). This classroom dialogue illustrates what happens when participants deconstruct language in the South Carolina Constitution:

> BREWER: Now let's look at number 3. [*she reads*] I am not an idiot, or insane, a pauper supported at public expense, or confined to any public prison. You check that. You're not an idiot. You're not insane and you're not a pauper. So this refers to any person who is insane or who is an idiot or who is supported at public expense.
>
> RESPONSE: If you were an idiot, you wouldn't know how to fill it out.
>
> BREWER: Huh? You wouldn't know how to fill it out? Well, we don't have to worry about that.[29]

Brewer continues to read each line as she instructs participants on what to put in each blank space. She asks participants to turn to the next pages. Here there is a list of "offenses" that voters must swear to never having been convicted of. During the demonstration, a man seeks clarity on the question about criminal convictions. An extended discussion follows about what it means to be "guilty" and to be "convicted" of a crime. Adding to the debate, someone requests clarity about another term. This initiates an intense discussion that unites the practice of witnessing with an academic experience connected to a larger context. It is useful to quote this exchange at length:

> BREWER: Let's turn over to the next page and look at that. We are running over time. We, we were late getting started. We will go over this then—on Tuesday night we will

define some of these things so that they will know what
it is. We have gone over those words one by one and
defined them so we will know what they are. [*she reads*] I
have never been convicted of any of the following crimes:
burglary, arson, obtaining goods or money under false
pretenses, perjury, forgery, robbery, bribery, adultery,
bigamy, wife beating, housebreaking, receiving stolen
goods, breach of trust with fraudulent intent, fornication,
sodomy, incest, assault with intent to ravish, miscegenation, larceny, or crimes against the election laws; or—.
Now, if you are not guilty of any of those, then you check
number 5. Have you been legally pardoned from such
conviction? That person may be guilty of some of those
crimes, but [if they] have served time or [been] sentenced
or paid a fine for, or they have been sentenced or pardoned, you're still a citizen.
PARTICIPANT 1: . . . guilty of those things and you have been
pardoned. Now, who are you asking? If the person hadn't
been pardoned, you wouldn't be asking them because
I'd be in jail. By being pardoned, it look like . . . if he
was guilty of those things he wouldn't qualify. Then if
you were pardoned, you would qualify? Then the reason
people can't vote is because you are guilty of those things?
You have to spend the time [in prison].
BREWER: And they'd have to be legally pardoned.
PARTICIPANT 1: . . . because if you spent the time you're not
legally threatening?
PARTICIPANT 2: . . . if you served time then you're *guilty*.
BREWER: There's a part of the law in the constitution of
South Carolina that refers to who has been pardoned for
a certain crime—that they are, it's no longer held against
them.
PARTICIPANT 1: . . . [*sarcastically*] kill people and sentenced for
a lifetime and sometimes are pardoned—now that's on
there, but they did not mention killing people, murder.

BREWER: I did read some place in the constitution where the person who has been legally pardoned, where the crime is no longer held against them.

PARTICIPANT 1: The only question I ask, is the thing that you have been actually guilty from, you don't have to be legally pardoned? You have paid the fine and spent the time. So after you spent the time, you are legally pardoned, you done spent the time. Now, I can see if the person done spent a lifetime in jail and he spent five or ten years then he is legally pardoned.

BREWER: Now I really don't think that the registration people search records to get that on the registrar when they come in, do you?

CLARK: After you read this thing. And, uh, to be able to check that, and if they check it and say that they are not guilty of these, there is then a search put on them.

PARTICIPANT 1: But we don't know that. It could be . . .

CLARK: It could be. You don't want to confuse all the people around, making them feel that statement applies to one person. That they really can't go down to get a registration certificate. I'm pretty sure they can go down and get their registration certificate.

PARTICIPANT 1: Just know that you're not guilty of those things.

BREWER: You know the law is a tricky thing. We might wrap ourselves up, but at the same time we might get the other person confused. And it is very confusing at times. If you go looking into the technicalities of some of these things. But our main aim is not to confuse you, but to get you on the registration books. Or to get you registered. If one has been legally pardoned for those crimes [it] is just as confusing as the first part of those statements, and actually I imagine they mean that if you have served time for that crime they consider that being legally pardoned. You are free to register and vote. So if you have served time for that crime, it would be hard to say that you have never been convicted of those crimes. I think it would be more in your rights in checking that part to say that you have been legally pardoned. Because so far as the law is concerned, now you are free. You have served your time.

PARTICIPANT 1: Yeah, that was the way I saw it. That if a person goes to jail to serve time or pays the fine. If they have served their time, then there are no longer anything held against them. And I considered that as being pardoned. Because you can't pay for a thing two ways.

BREWER: We would like to say to those persons who are filling this out that we would like you to come back on Tuesday. We go further into this. And to help you to fill this blank out yourself. And then on to more blanks.[30]

In addition to using writing exercises to help illuminate the actual definitions and break down the stigma attached to terms, participants hold a discussion about terms, gaining power and control over dominant oppressive language: this is an act of *Nommo*—actualizing the unity between spiritual and material aspects of existence. In this particular session, Brewer attempts to guide the discussion toward ways to complete the application, emphasizing that participants should just check off this section and move on. But the participants are not willing to pass over the "words" with minimal concern. Words matter, and they know it.

This dialogue shows participants questioning language traditionally used to disenfranchise African American people. The participants raise questions about this language, demonstrating a grassroots level of intellectual consciousness. They ask questions about the terms, and they take the time to express their thoughts and understanding about a larger social subject, the criminal justice system. They are demonstrating the value and meaning of civic inclusion, but also the value of knowledge and the importance of understanding these terms. The term *pardoned,* for example, carries significant social and political implications. Participants don't just accept a quick definition of the term. They discuss what it means to them, what it means to the registrar, and what it means to the State of South Carolina. In this exchange, this is the only place where Brewer is not clear about the material she is teaching. Characteristically, she includes herself as a learner, engaging the help of Septima Clark and the class to determine the meaning for themselves.

5

"And Still I Rise": Finding Redemption through Unceasing Variations of Literacy Acquisition and Use

> We are a people. A people do not throw their geniuses away. And if they are thrown away, it is our duty as artists and as witnesses for the future to collect them again for the sake of our children, and, if necessary, bone by bone.
>
> Alice Walker, *In Search of Our Mothers' Gardens*

WHEN BERNICE ROBINSON ARRIVED FOR THE first night of Citizenship School classes, she was ready to do whatever it took to initiate and sustain the program. She could not know, however, that her efforts would become the organizational roots from which the entire Civil Rights Movement would eventually branch out and grow into the Freedom Schools—the engines of the voter registration work throughout the South. Questions still linger in African American historical accounts: how could she understand that fifty years later, in major urban neighborhoods, her model would stand as an example for charter schools and adult education programs? As she prepared that first lesson, she could not have known that while she was crucial to the development of the program, she would rarely be mentioned in the history of African American intellectual development, and that her creative critical thinking efforts would never be recognized in the grand narrative of the Civil Rights Movement. She could not have known that the instructional material she prepared for that first night would not come close to satisfying the immense intellectual hunger of those attending the first class. She could not have known the immeasurable desire of local preachers' wives, beauticians, and domestic and social workers to learn how to teach writing. Foremost, she could not have imagined that the learners' motivations beyond voter registration and civic inclusion offered access to the "tree of life." Did she know that participants experienced deep emotional passion in learning to write because it meant being able to communicate with sons and daughters who had moved away? Did she know what was at stake in the absence of those tools, such as the ability to sign one's name on property deeds passed down for three generations? Or that literacy acquisition meant being able to write items and numbers on a postal money order to purchase items from the Sears, Roebuck catalog, avoiding the humiliation of race-based ignorance occurring in local retail stores? (Jim Crow ideology enforced a humiliation tactic that prohibited a black woman from trying on a hat or other garment prior to purchase.) Or did Robinson's hopes for the program outweigh all her thoughts of inadequacy or unpreparedness, with an eye toward the full fruit of a labor of love—aspirations firmly planted in the ideology of literacy and all it would bring: civic inclusion, freedom, autonomy, prosperity, equality? Did she understand the ancestral Sea Islands belief that the harvest always blooms in the right season? Imagine Robinson's optimism as she learned from learners how to teach them what they wanted to learn, laughing with them at the mere idea of remedial writing material, which she immediately revised according to their instructions. Imagine Robinson's pleasure in learning that voter registration was not the only reason they participated and that more practical writing applications should motivate the program's curriculum. Whatever she knew or didn't know, on January 7, 1957, Bernice V. Robinson went about the business of building a curriculum that represented these desires.

Finding redemption is the overarching theme of gospel literacy. It's a theoretical interpretive concept centered on recovery, a means of dispelling the myth of grassroots literacy acquisition and use as basic, simple, or mechanical. Participants like Bernice Robinson embody the relationship between literacy and redemption. Her literacy activism exemplifies the goal of restoring to a place of honor the critical intellectual activism driving both secular and sacred practices. Finding redemption is here a means of exploring and explaining how intense spiritual and cultural ways of being work as literacy activism in a political context.

BERNICE ROBINSON: "DISTURBING THE ELEMENTS"

Establishing Robinson as an example of redemption carries with it the need to look at how she defined the scope and possibilities of her literacy activism. By insisting on having a place in the history of the Citizenship Schools, Robinson internalized and engaged in a "finding redemption" ideology. She reclaimed her crucial contribution to the schools by revising the slate of activities—family and community—specific to her own literacy story. She was well aware of her absence in historical accounts of this literacy event. During a 1979 interview celebrating Highlander's fiftieth anniversary, historians Sue Thrasher and Eliot Wigginton asked Robinson to tell her literacy story, and afterward she was given a draft of the interview transcript, Robinson's transformation of current consciousness manifested not only in the way she recovered (redeemed) her involvement, but also in offering a theory about the cause of her marginalization. She responded:

> As you so ably expressed in the later section of your manuscript, there is not much of a record of my entire involvement. The reason for this is that I never did much talking about the many areas in which I have been involved and then too, very rarely does anyone interview me when they are seeking information about the Citizenship Training Program and those who developed this program. I have often wondered why I have been excluded when I really consider this program, the greatest challenge and achievement of my life. (Robinson n.d.)[1]

Andrew Young's assertion in the epigraph of the introduction indicates that the Civil Rights Movement showcased a diversity of race, class, and gender. During the Civil Rights era, great numbers of African American people—locally, nationally, and internationally

—in their own way took the lead in the struggle for human dignity. Sea Islands organizers such as Mary Lee Davis, Ethel Grimball, and Aileen Brewer were leaders willing to forfeit their livelihood in order to fight against racial oppression and discrimination. Finding redemption requires reconciliation and reaffirmation, and being bold enough to pay attention to minds, hearts, souls, and experiences for the purpose of recovering language that is rooted in the desire to teach in a way that deeply affects others. Redemption embodies Alice Walker's notion, expressed in the chapter-opening epigraph, that people have an obligation to recover instances of brilliance.

Robinson took control of restoring her literacy story when historians questioned her about her first literacy memory. She chose to begin by explaining the source of her identity, a link between her first memory of learning and a peach tree. After a long struggle with a life-threatening illness that rendered her unconscious, Robinson woke up to her first memories—the blossoms on a peach tree, learning to walk, and then starting school. These memories segue into her recovery of health and education:

> Before I started first grade. Before I started into kindergarten and I don't remember anything much about it [life before school]. The only thing I can remember about it [life] was when I looked out the window and I saw the blossoms on the peach tree in the backyard and I got out of the bed to go downstairs to play because I used to like to feel the blossoms off the peach tree falling all over me. (Thrasher and Wigginton Interview)

For Robinson the peach tree memory is part of redeeming her literacy acquisition. Like knowledge, memory emerges from the dim reaches of our consciousness. Most people can pinpoint images that have a privileged position in their life stories. And while early memories often have the vague characteristics of a dream, some include the vivid clarity of a photograph. Robinson's first memory of her gateway to literacy is prefaced by a mysterious fascination with the blossoms of a peach tree that have come to symbolize her life and literacy. And so her literacy story goes. . . .

Bernice Violanthe Robinson was born on February 7, 1914, a date also recorded as the first time in more than 100 years it had snowed in Charleston. Robinson believed that being born during the snowfall meant she was born to "disturb the elements." Toward the end of a long struggle with a life-threatening illness, the doctors gave up treating her, preparing her parents for her imminent death. Although her frail five-year-old body was overcome with infection and fever, her mother refused to give up: she began the ritual of wrapping a sick child in a blanket filled with sliced onions.. Robinson recalled the rancid smell of onions peeled and wrapped in a blanket around her fevered body. Paramount here is the vision of her mother's unrelenting love, reclaiming her daughter through steadfast faithfulness.

Memory itself can be considered composition. We continually—often unconsciously—revise our memories, rewriting them into stories that bring coherence to chaos. Composing memory is the ultimate intellectual activity because it continually seeks meaning in the random and often unfathomable events of our lives. Robinson's memory composes and contains her literacy history, which speaks volumes about her life more broadly: heart, soul, and mind. Perhaps the starting point in her narrative is like the creation stories that humans tell about the origins of the earth: *This is who I am because this is how I began.* Giving special attention to illogical, supernatural, spiritual, or otherwise unexplainable events puts the unexpected, unpredictable incidents and directions of our lives into perspective. Often the memories with the most emotional impact are those we don't really understand, the images that rise up in unexpected circumstances. For Bernice Robinson, these are literacy/writing instruction, snow, the peach tree, and her literacy story. These are the highlights of her repository of memories that she holds in her heart and her head, memories recovered as part of her access to learning. Through a redemption ethos—another chance at life—we can recover the details necessary to describe more than the surface events of our lives; redemption is also a means of making intuitive connections to articulate a truth that cannot be directly spoken. Thus, Bernice Robinson's practice of literacy activism allows us to see more deeply into the significance and redemptive aspects of literacy learning and use for African American Sea Islands residents during the Civil Rights era.

Robinson's understanding of literacy as a means of finding redemption goes beyond the Christian ideology of life in the hereafter. For Robinson redemption is the means toward a teaching and learning narrative, one in which life and learning are interchangeable. As she tells the story of her own learning, she doesn't begin with an explanation of how she learned to use a pencil, recite the alphabet, or memorize multiplication tables. She makes a conscious choice to begin with a story of how her body was dangerously infected and how she recovered from a near-death experience. Robinson combines the learning question asked by the researchers with her vision/memory and relationship with a peach tree. She's well aware that the interviewers are academic historians writing a book about Highlander Folk School and the Citizenship Education Program, and that her response should be based on her material, pedagogical contribution. Yet she makes a conscious decision to record in her literacy narrative her earliest life memory—her interaction with a peach tree, clearly a symbol of life—so that she can harmoniously find redemption, a necessary part of life. Robinson describes her literacy recovery through an experience with a peach tree as it cycles through its ultimate stage of development: shedding to facilitate growth. Ultimately, Robinson defines her initial opportunity to learn—in kindergarten and first grade—through that tree, which works as both a spiritual and a physical way of knowing in which her thinking, understanding, and reasoning combine with her feelings. Robinson understands literacy and life as embodied. Perhaps at five or six years old, she knew the importance of the "family tree" metaphor in African American culture. And maybe she understood the game little girls play of attempting to catch a leaf or blossom as it falls from a tree, prompting recovery from death.

Literacy practices are commonplace in most grassroots activism. Bernice Robinson often repeated the story of her initial teaching experience to teacher trainees, educators, and historians. She often testified at university lectures halls and political campaign rallies. In 1967, Robinson implemented the gospel literacy practice of bearing witness as a means of inspiring the participants of a weeklong symposium on economic opportunity at the University of Wisconsin. She distinctly acknowledged the burden to everyone from Chattanooga beauticians to literacy conference attendees at Cabrillo College in California. In 1972 she told her story during her political campaign—she was the first African American woman to run for a seat in the South Carolina House of Representatives. That her contribution to the Civil Rights Movement was ignored caused her considerable anguish as she came to realize how much of her hard work lay in the shadow of her more educated and prolific cousin Septima Clark, an agony that Robinson humbly expressed during an interview with Highlander historians in 1979. One wonders why she was excluded from the records as a developer of the Citizenship Schools. She asked, "Why doesn't anyone ever interview me when they are seeking information about the Citizenship Training Program?" Why indeed, Mrs. Robinson?

Bernice Robinson's life history prompts one question: how did a self-taught woman with no formal training in composition studies, particularly writing, develop a curriculum that directly or indirectly trained every teacher associated with the Student Non-violent Coordinating Committee, the Congress of Racial Equality, and the Southern Christian Leadership Conference; transcended race, gender, class, and religious ideologies; and lasted three generations? If we pay attention, her literacy acquisition and use answer this question. She responded to the needs of real people in local communities. Community-based literacy practices and events, both teaching and learning, provide access to redemptive literacy narratives, which identify and then break free of limits on literacy activism. Robinson's literacy story recovers the breadth and depth of the collective efforts of African Americans both before and during the Civil Rights era. Citizenship School participants were local, self-taught people who combined critical thinking strategies with deeply held beliefs to make literacy practices central to their fight against racial, economic, and gender oppression.[2] The limitations on literacy activism occurred primarily because challenges in writing instruction—acquisition and use—were often attributed to factors such as motivation, methods, and means, when they very well might have been the result of asymmetry between instruction and the learners' objectives, values, or purpose. The concept of redemption is a mechanism by which composition studies can address the value of such symmetry once its existence has been identified in grassroots literacy practices. Finding redemption, then, operates on a sacred–secular continuum, calling on principles of spirituality—hope, faith, love, and courage—through expressions of intellectual power and authority. For the Citizenship School participants, literacy was not reduced to a secular or cognitive activity; it was connected to their most deeply held beliefs about the spiritual source of their strength.

Gospel literacy is a ritual of critical intellectualism that relies on sophisticated ways of knowing. In the context of composition and rhetoric, this includes conducting class discussions that help in the recovery of African American cultural traditions, restoring grassroots African American people to the status of "agents of change," not victims of oppression and dominance (Royster, *Traces* 253). *Freedom Writing* recovers the ways in which Citizenship School participants—teachers and learners alike—bore witness to their own intellectual value, thus delivering *themselves* from evil through the acquisition and use of knowledge and redemption forever.

My efforts of recovery through this book are aimed toward one goal: if I can link the grassroots literacy activities of the African American Civil Rights Movement to contemporary literacy issues, then many troubled students in community literacy programs, especially black women who are otherwise at risk for harmful activities, might identify with these ordinary grassroots heroines and focus their energies in a creative direction. Teaching, research, writing, and activism, along with university-sponsored community literacy programs devoted to uplifting the entire black community, can facilitate this objective.

~Amen

Introduction: The Gospel According to Literacy

1. In this project, I use the terms *African* and *black American* inter-changeably to discuss individuals of African descent born in the United States of America. These terms are also used interchangeably in the ERIC and JSTOR databases to describe this same group.

2. Ultimately I believe that we enrich our perspective when we consid-er literate practices across generations, geographies, and educational and cultural lines, as well as across socioeconomic locations.

3. Alice Wine, as quoted in *Ain't You Got a Right to the Tree of Life? The People of Johns Island, South Carolina—Their Faces, Their Words, and Their Songs*, edited by Guy Carawan and Candie Carawan (149). This published work is a collection of excerpts from oral histories with Johns Island residents. Folk singers Guy and Candie Carawan conducted the initial interviews in 1968. In 1989 they returned to the island to conduct additional interviews. This revised edition includes excerpts from both sets of interviews.

4. Gilyard, in "Introduction: Aspects of African American Rhetoric as a Field," offers an extensive treatment of Marcus Hanna Boulware's analysis of black rhetoric. Gospel literacy, defined in the next sec-tion, has similar motives: (1) to protest grievances, (2) to state com-plaints, (3) to demand rights, (4) to advocate for racial cooperation, (5) to mold racial consciousness, and (6) to stimulate racial pride.

5. Unpublished, uncataloged Robinson papers, Avery Research Cen-ter. Charleston, South Carolina, 2005.

6. Unpublished Robinson interview with Sandra Oldendorf, January 12, 1986.

7. Anderson Mack interview with the author, Wadmalaw Island, South Carolina, November 9, 2000.

8. To date, literacy studies has explored the methods, motivations, and materials that grassroots advocates developed for learning to read,

write, or explicitly teach those skills as a means of combating oppressive ideologies or engaging in literacy activism.

9. See also Besnier's introduction to *Literacy, Emotion, and Authority: Reading and Writing on a Polynesian Atoll.*

10. Brandt's perspective in *Literacy in American Lives* is useful because she calls attention to the dilemma within social historical studies that struggles to clarify connections between literacy learning and larger systems. She sees social historians confronting a more convoluted dilemma because of the difficulty in applying these theories; one factor tends to compete with another. Brandt explains, "Revisionist historians try to recover the broader contexts that favored or disfavored literacy in particular times and places" (27). She warns that "blanket claims about the causes of literacy are extremely difficult to apply" (27).

11. For more on New Literacy studies, see Brian Street's "The New Literacy Studies" in Cushman, Kintgen, Kroll, and Rose. See also Anderson; Graff (*Labyrinths, Literacy*); Heath; and Kaestle, Damon-Moore, Stedman, Tinsley, and Trollinger.

12. For more on this, see J. D. Anderson.

13. Works including those of Cushman et al.; Graff (*Labyrinths, Literacy*); Kaestle et al.; and Lunsford, Moglen, and Slevin place the study of literacy within contexts that include religion, education, political ideology, criminality, and economic development. Sylvia Scribner and Michael Cole in *The Psychology of Literacy* contribute to our understanding of the relationships between literacy, culture, and cognitive development, illustrating that complicated meanings of literacy are understood best when considered in a specific social, economic, or political context.

1. Like a Bridge over Troubled Water

1. Historians cite the mid-1790s as the formation of the first black Baptist Church, located in Silver Bluff, South Carolina, on the land later disputed in the Galphin Affair, under the leadership of David George, an African American minister. For an account of Colonial African American religious practices, see Jon Butler, *Awash in a Sea of Faith: Christianizing the American People* (Cambridge: Harvard UP, 1990, 149–63); John B. Boles, *Masters and Slaves in the House of the Lord: Race and Religion in the American South, 1740–1870* (Lexington: UP of Kentucky, 1988); and Albert J. Raboteau, *Slave Religion, The "Invisible Institution" in the Antebellum South* (New York: Oxford UP, 1978).

2. Anthony Heilbut writes a complete history of African American gospel music in his book *The Gospel Sound: Good News and Bad Times*.

3. My use of gospel concepts as a theoretical framework originates in various works by Craig Werner (*Change, Higher, Playing*), who tracks the social and political achievements of artists such as Aretha Franklin, Stevie Wonder, Curtis Mayfield, and James Baldwin. In his work, Werner joins African American soul, blues, and jazz music to describe a way of life rather than solely a musical form. Through my reading of Werner's work, I connect the spirit of a gospel vision to literacy, thus developing gospel literacy.

4. From a note card in the unarchived Robinson collection.

5. I use the term *African* as a general designation; however, I acknowledge the multiple and diverse cultures on the African continent.

6. Bernice Reagon is a civil rights activist, an accomplished Freedom singer, and founder of the musical group Sweet Honey in the Rock.

7. I use the term *history* instead of *knowledge* because I want to represent a ritual taking place over time, not simply a moment or event.

8. Moss illustrates how African ministers use general testimonies to create similar communal bonds (*Community* 63).

9. I use the terms *witnessing* and *testimony* interchangeably. Both concepts, in black discourse, involve telling stories of divine intervention. For a more extensive discussion on the intersections of these terms, see Rosetta Ross's *Witnessing and Testifying: Black Women, Religion, and the Civil Rights Movement*.

10. See also K. Williams and Gilyard ("Introduction"). Smitherman further explains that "all activities of men, and all the movements in nature, rest on the word, on the productive power of the word, which is water and heat and seed and Nommo, that is life force itself[,] . . . the force, responsibility, and commitment of the word, and the awareness that the word alone alters the world" (*Talkin' and Testifyin'* 78). Smitherman goes on to explain the critical foundation and role of *Nommo* in African culture, stating: "In traditional African culture, a newborn child's a mere thing until his father speaks his name. No medicine, potion, or magic of any sort is considered effective without accompanying words. So strong is the African belief in the power of absolute necessity of Nommo that all craftsmanship must be accompanied by speech" (78). It's also important to note that Smitherman and Gilyard are not alone in conceptualizing *Nommo* as an instrumental power in the African American community. Maulana Karenga and Molefi Asante have both done extensive

work describing *Nommo* as an African-derived communication concept.

11. This idea draws on the intellectual debates of liberal thinkers like John Dewey who were in search of a civic faith that would guide the United States. Dewey desired for secular contexts the positive attributes of religious faith such as self-giving, altruism, self-sacrifice, and discipline (see Chappell).

2. "Gonna Lay Down My Burdens"

1. Better indicators of economic security are race, gender, and class.
2. Ultimately, Freirean educational philosophy dictates that when people take control of their history, the role of education changes. See his conversation with Myles Horton in *We Make the Road by Walking: Conversations on Education and Social Change* in the section titled "The People Begin to Get Their History into Their Hands, and Then the Role of Education Changes" (215–67).
3. See Royster (*Traces* 265). People who "do intellectual work" need to understand their intellectual ancestry.
4. It's important to note that illiterate white people also felt the impact of the literacy tests, since some of the understanding and grandfather clauses expired after a few years, and some whites were reluctant to expose their illiteracy by publicly resorting to these clauses.
5. In Mississippi, applicants had to submit a written statement on what the vote meant to them and explain why they should be allowed to gain it, and then persuade the county registrar that they had an adequate understanding of citizenship under a constitutional form of government (see Payne; K. Branch).
6. See Payne; Johnson.
7. "A Proposal for the Citizenship School Training Program." General reports and memoranda, 1960–1962. Wisconsin Historical Society, Highlander Research and Education Center Collection, Box 38, File 2.
8. During this period, Septima Clark documented information about the Citizenship Schools on the Sea Islands in two reports intended for the Highlander Folk School and the Schwarzhaupt Foundation. The "Citizenship Program" report is handwritten and documents enrollment, participant ages, and results for each of the Sea Islands' Citizenship Schools between December 1958 and February 26, 1959. The "Sea Islands Program" is typed and documents cumulative enrollment and results for the Sea Islands Citizenship Schools between January and February 1959. I have used these reports to

construct my description of the program. However, there are some notable discrepancies. For example, Clark documents 100 participants in the "Citizenship Program" report and 106 participants in the "Sea Island Program" report. In addition, she records 51 new registrants in 1959 in the "Citizenship Program" report and 56 in the "Sea Islands Program" report. Where there are discrepancies, I have used the data in the "Sea Islands Program" report, as Tjerandsen, David Levine, and Oldendorf ("Highlander," "Literacy") have done. See Septima P. Clark, "Citizenship Program—Statistical Reports on Adult Schools in Alabama, Georgia, and South Carolina (1960–1961)," Highlander Research and Education Center, Box 3, Folder 8; Septima P. Clark, "Sea Islands Program from January 1 to July, 1959," Box 49, Folder 9. For references to the "Sea Islands Program" report, see Tjerandsen's *Education for Citizenship,* page 167.

9. Robinson, unpublished manuscript "Reaching Out: Empowerment of the Estranged, the Powerless," Avery Research Center for African American History and Culture, Bernice Robinson Collection, Box 4.

10. See also Bernice Robinson quoted in Wigginton, *Refuse to Stand Silently By* (249); Clark, *Echo in My Soul* (144) and *Ready from Within* (47). The Progressive Club altered the economic balance on Johns Island. When residents purchased groceries and other goods at the Progressive Club store, their money stayed within the community. They avoided the inflated prices and credit practices of white-owned businesses. In the cooperative store, African American customers did not stand aside while white customers received the clerk's uninterrupted attention, nor were black customers expected to respond respectfully when white clerks refused to refer to them as "Mr." or "Mrs." In addition, they used the profits from the store to repay the loan from Highlander and eventually owned the building outright (Clark, *Ready from Within* 47; Tjerandsen 160).

11. Don West left Highlander in 1933.

12. The SCLC replaced Highlander headquarters as the program's home; teacher training moved to southeastern Georgia; Clark relocated with the program from Monteagle to Atlanta to join new staff members Andrew Young and Dorothy Cotton; Bernice Robinson remained at Highlander; and the American Missionary Association (AMA) provided administrative oversight. Despite these changes, Robinson and Clark walked the new recruits through training sessions. At the end of the week, participants stated that they felt the

workshop did for them what the Citizenship School did for the students. It revealed the individual responsibility in first-class citizenship and gave them the courage to assume this responsibility and to work actively in community development (Robinson, Olendorf Interview). In his biography, Andrew Young described the SCLC leadership's initial response to the Citizenship Education Program as lukewarm, explaining, "In the beginning, it must be said that our project was not taken very seriously by the SCLC board and many of SCLC's prominent preachers." Clark also "was often frustrated." Young wrote that he "was content to spend [his] energy on training rather than engage in struggles for recognition within the organization" (Young 144).

13. Wisconsin Historical Society, Highlander Research and Education Center Collection.

14. Emil Schwarzhaupt was a German who immigrated to the United States in 1910, making millions in the liquor business (Tjerandsen).

3. "I Got Some Pride"

1. "Transcription of a meeting at the home of Mrs. Septima P. Clark in Charleston, SC," February 17, 1959. Highlander Research and Education Center Collection, New Market, TN, Box 3, Folder 4.

2. In 1966, Guy and Candie Carawan used their position as Highlander staff to collect narratives from Johns Island, South Carolina. Their work resulted in a book that documents the words and songs of the island from 1953 to 1966. In the following pages, unless otherwise noted, quotes from Esau Jenkins can be found in Guy Carawan and Candie Carawan's *Ain't You Got a Right to the Tree of Life: The People of Johns Island, South Carolina, Their Faces, Their Words, and Their Songs.*

3. Anderson Mack, another Citizenship School participant, identified this as a primary reason for not beginning his schooling until the age of eleven.

4. Robinson 1979 interview on videotape Reel 1, Highlander Research and Education Center Collection, New Market, TN. (See also H. Williams).

5. Ibid.

6. Bernice Robinson, Avery archives.

7. For more on the role of beauty shops in African American political culture, see Kathy Peiss, *Hope in a Jar: The Making of America's Beauty Culture* (New York: Metropolitan Books, 1998), 89–95, 257; Evelyn Newman Phillips, "Doing More Than Heads: African

American Women Healing, Resisting, and Uplifting Others in St. Petersburg, Florida" (*Frontiers* 22, 2001), 25–42; Julie A. Willett, *Permanent Waves: The Making of the American Beauty Shop* (New York: New York UP, 2000), 3–4, 131–35.

8. See Bernice Robinson Collection, Avery Research Center for African American History and Culture, Charleston, South Carolina, Box 1, Folder 2.

9. Robinson considered herself a member of the group, and in most of her narratives she hesitates to refer to participants as "students." Instead, when she talks about them, she uses their given names and, during instructional sessions or when reflecting back, she calls them "people."

10. Bernice Reagon's perspective on call-and-response helps me to demonstrate how teaching and learning affirm or present an alternate perspective on an initial call.

11. Orlando Patterson describes the fundamental essence of personal freedom for oppressed people: "[Personal freedom,] at its most elementary, gives a person the sense that one, on the one hand, is not being coerced or restrained by another person in doing something desired and, on the other hand, the conviction that one can do as one pleases within the limits of other persons' desire to do the same" (3).

12. Letters from Citizenship School students to the Highland Folk School in 1959, Wisconson Historical Society, Highlander Research and Education Center Collection, Box 67, Files 5 and 9.

13. Andrews supports this theory when defining the value of literacy to nineteenth-century African Americans, stating that "autobiography became a very public way of declaring oneself free, or redefining freedom and then assigning it to oneself in defiance of one's bonds to the past or the social, political and sometimes even the moral exigencies of the present" (xi). Most enslaved African Americans were able to observe the political power of those who could read and write. They were clearly aware of their disenfranchisement and believed that becoming literate in the language of the oppressors would give them the opportunity to govern themselves. This belief was passed down through generations and became a primary focus of the twentieth-century literacy crusade.

14. "Workshop on Training Leaders for Citizenship Schools," January 19–21, 1961; Wisconsin Historical Society, Box 4, Folder 15, HFS, p. 1. This report is a partial transcript of the workshop discussions.

15. Ibid.

16. Citizenship School participants responded to the early classes. Some of the comments were on tape and some wrote letters. Wisconsin Historical Society, Box 67, Folders 9 and 5.

17. Ibid.

18. Illiteracy also existed among whites on the island, according to Mack.

19. Anderson Mack interviewed by the author, Wadmalaw Island, November 9, 2000.

4. "I've Got a Testimony"

1. "Training Workshop," Wisconsin Historical Society: Tape 515A no. 51. August 9, 1961. Septima led a discussion on how to set up a Citizenship School.

2. The initial curriculum, found in the student workbooks, was developed from the materials Robinson put together during the first Citizenship School sessions.

3. In this discussion, *witnessing* and *testifying* are interchangeable terms. Within an Afrocentric ideology, to testify is to bear witness.

4. Tape 807A (1957) (Wisconsin Historical Society) contains recordings of the final class during the first Citizenship School (on Johns Island). Between November 1954 and May 1961, Myles and Zilphia Horton visited the Sea Islands. Zilphia, an anthropologist, attended local Citizenship Classes; she carried a camera and tape recorder on these trips for the purpose of documenting Highlander efforts in the area (see Tjerandsen [4]; Adams (*Unearthing* [84–88]).

5. Citizenship Education Pamphlet *My Reading Booklet 1958–1959,* Wisconsin Historical Society, Box 67, Folder 10. The booklet was later used in all the Citizenship Schools and subsequent Freedom Schools. It was modified to meet the particular needs of various southern states. The purpose of the booklet was also modified to fit the goals of the sponsoring organization.

6. Anderson Mack interview with the author, Wadmalaw Island, November 9, 2000. All quotations from Mack in this chapter derive from this interview.

7. *My Citizenship Booklet* (1961–62). Highlander Research and Education Center, Box 2, Folders 25 and 25.

8. Here I find Ladson-Billings's perspective on a critically conscious curriculum useful. She argues that unlike critical pedagogy, culturally relevant pedagogy embraces the principle of critical consciousness, which includes a collective component that is equally com-

mitted to individual and collective empowerment ("But That's Just Good Teaching!" 160).

9. *My Citizenship Booklet 1959–1960*, Highlander Research and Education Center.

10. Another teaching tool used in the early classes was a pamphlet entitled "Why Vote? The ABC's of Citizenship" (1958). This pamphlet was published by the Channing L. Bete Co., Inc., in Greenfield, Massachusetts. Its simple layout includes cartoons intended to reinforce the message that every vote counts (see the pamphlet's appendix). However, included on page 2 is the statement "Did you know that the word Idiot comes from a Greek word meaning the Man who didn't vote?" In an attempt to invoke humor, the pamphlet also emphasizes five primary ideas intended to motivate learners to participate in voter registration: (1) know the issues, (2) recognize that local issues are as important as state or national ones, (3) look beyond campaign promises, (4) get involved in local politics, and (5) work together to accomplish change. (Wisconsin Historical Society, "Why Vote: The ABC's of Citizenship" [1958], Box 38 Folder 14.)

11. Later classes included lessons on handling the press and publicity, organizing mass meetings, and getting speakers.

12. Unidentified speech in Robinson papers, "Political Education/ Working with Blacks in Rural South Carolina," Bernice V. Robinson Papers, 1920–1989, Avery Research Center.

13. Second Step Voter Education Schools, 1963–65. Wisconsin Historical Society, Box 68, Folders 1 and 6.

14. Wisconsin Historical Society, Tape 807A, No. 53. August 10, 1961.

15. Ethel J. Grimball interview by Sandra Oldendorf, January 30, 1987, Charleston, South Carolina.

16. The Wadmalaw classes were held in a small building belonging to the Presbyterian Church.

17. Dorothy Cotton also gives a detailed account to Eliot Wigginton in *Refuse to Stand Silently By: An Oral History of Grass Roots Social Activism in America, 1921–64* (New York: Doubleday, 1991), 285.

18. Wisconsin Historical Society, Tape 515A, No. 53 (1961), Sides 1 and 2, unidentified participant. Citizenship School teachers discuss methods.

19. Wisconsin Historical Society, Tape 515A, No. 53 (August 10, 1961). This Citizenship training session included a demonstration of teaching reading and writing, comments on and criticisms of methods used in the demonstration, discussion of procedures em-

ployed in grouping students and selecting teachers for the school, and responsibilities of supervisors and teachers. A symbiotic relationship is at work here. What happens when we problematize teaching to be a co-relationship, and what does that mean for people who need to be in control?

20. Wisconsin Historical Society, Box 82, File Folder 7. Unpublished document by Aimee Horton, "Analysis of Programs," 97.

21. Participant letter by Solomon Brown. Fifteen participants wrote letters to their teachers and Highlander Folk School in 1957. Participant responses from the early classes were positive. Ten student reactions were recorded on tape. Wisconsin Historical Society, Box 67, Folders 9 and 5.

22. Wisconsin Historical Society, Tape 515A, No. 44.

23. Wisconsin Historical Society, Tape 807A (1957).

24. Ibid.

25. This is the Freirean idea of naming what people want to learn as the first step in knowing.

26. Revisions for popular tunes were common. For example, to the tune of "My Darling Clementine," Robinson taught participants the words, "Who's the grandest guy in the world?—Myles Horton." She also changed the words in "Soldiers of the Cross" to "We are building a better nation through this school. And each voter makes us stronger." Interview with Oldendorf, Tape 807A (1957).

27. Carawan interview by author (2000); Tape 515A (1960), Wisconsin Historical Society.

28. Ibid.

29. Ibid.

30. Ibid.

5. "And Still I Rise"

1. From a notecard in the unarchived Robinson collection.

2. See Heather Andrea Williams, who traces the intense desire of enslaved people to become literate, demonstrating how they acquired skills on their own initiative rather than by formal instruction.

BIBLIOGRAPHY

Archival collections are more fluid than one might expect of historical documents. Over the course of my research, collections I consulted sometimes found a new home and institutions sometimes changed names. To help other researchers who are interested in tracking down material on the subject of this book, in the notes and works cited sections I have provided the last-known home of specific documents, which isn't always where I found them. Many of the materials I consulted that are now found in the Bernice Robinson Collection, for instance, were not archived when I accessed them, which is why not all of the source citation notes include box and file numbers. Most of the materials are currently in one of two places: the Wisconsin Historical Society and the Highlander Research and Education Center. Many of the latter's archives now reside in the former. Following is a list of the archival collections I consulted.

Bernice Robinson Collection, Avery Research Center for African American History and Culture, Charleston, South Carolina.

Citizenship Education Program Collection, SCLC Archives, Martin Luther King, Jr. Center for Non-Violent Change, Atlanta, Georgia.

Esau Jenkins Collection, Avery Research Center for African American History and Culture, Charleston, South Carolina.

Highlander Library, Highlander Research and Education Center, New Market, Tennessee.

Highlander Research and Education Center Collection, Wisconsin Historical Society, Madison, Wisconsin.

Septima Clark Collection, Avery Research Center for African American History and Culture, Charleston, South Carolina.

Adams, Frank. "Highlander Folk School: Getting Information, Going Back and Teaching It." *Harvard Educational Review* 42.4 (1972): 497–520. Print.

Adams, Frank, with Myles Horton. *Unearthing Seeds of Fire: The Idea of Highlander.* Winston-Salem: Blair, 1975. Print.

Alkebulan, Adisa A. "The Spiritual Essence of African American Rhetoric." *Understanding African American Rhetoric: Classical Origins to Contemporary Innovations.* Ed. Ronald L. Jackson II and Elaine B. Richardson. New York: Routledge, 2003. 23–40. Print.

Anderson, J. D. "Literacy and Education in the African-American Experience." *Literacy among African-American Youth: Issues in Learning, Teaching and Schooling.* Ed. Vivian L. Gadsden and Daniel A. Wagner. Cresskill: Hampton, 1995. 19–37. Print.

Andrews, William L. *To Tell a Free Story: The First Century of Afro-American Autobiography, 1760–1865.* Champaign: U of Illinois P, 1986. Print.

Arnove, Robert F., and Harvey J. Graff. "National Literacy Campaigns." Cushman, Kintgen, Kroll, and Rose 591–615.

Asante, Molefi Kete. "The Afrocentric Idea in Education." *Journal of Negro Education* 60.2 (1991): 170–80. Print.

———. *The Afrocentric Idea Revised.* Philadelphia: Temple UP, 1998. Print.

Banks, Adam J. *Digital Griots: African American Rhetoric in a Multimedia Age.* Carbondale: Southern Illinois UP, 2011. Print.

Besnier, Niko. *Literacy, Emotion, and Authority: Reading and Writing on a Polynesian Atoll.* Cambridge: Cambridge UP, 1995. Print.

Branch, Kirk. "From the Margins at the Center: Literacy, Authority, and the Great Divide." *College Composition and Communication* 50.2 (1998): 206–31. Print.

Branch, Taylor. *Parting the Waters: America in the King Years, 1954–63.* New York: Simon, 1988. Print.

Brandt, Deborah. *Literacy in American Lives.* Cambridge: Cambridge UP, 2001. Print.

———. "Sponsors of Literacy." *College Composition and Communication* 49.2 (1998): 165–85. Print.

Brewer, Aileen. "Factual Report of Adult School." N.d. Box 38, Folder 3. Highlander Research and Education Center Collection, Wisconsin Historical Society, Madison, WI. Print.

———. "Final Report of the Edisto Adult School for 1959–1960." March 1960. Box 67, Folder 4. Highlander Research and Education Center Collection, Wisconsin Historical Society, Madison, WI. Print.

Brown, Cynthia Stokes, ed. *Ready from Within: Septima Clark and the Civil Rights Movement.* Navarro: Wild Trees, 1986. Print.

Carawan, Guy. "Report of Sea Islands Work." Box 8, Folder 9. Highlander Research and Education Center Collection. Wisconsin Historical Society, Madison, WI. Print.

Carawan, Guy, and Candie Carawan, eds. *Ain't You Got a Right to the Tree of Life? The People of Johns Island, South Carolina—Their Faces, Their Words, and Their Songs.* Rev. and expd. ed. Photos. Robert Yellin. New York: Simon, 1989. Print.

———. *Sing for Freedom: The Story of the Civil Rights Movement through Its Songs.* Bethlehem: Sing Out, 1990. Print.

Carawan, Guy, and Candie Carawan. Interview by Rhea Estelle Lathan. 11–15 Nov. 2000.

———. Interview by Sue Thrasher. Highlander Research and Education Center, New Market, TN. 28 Jan. 1982. Tape recording.

Chappell, David L. *A Stone of Hope: Prophetic Religion and the Death of Jim Crow.* Chapel Hill: U of North Carolina P, 2004. Print.

"Citizenship School Workbook." Atlanta: Southern Christian Leadership Conference, n.d. Box 2, Folder 25 and 26. Highlander Research and Education Center Collection. Wisconsin Historical Society, Madison, WI. Print.

Clark, Septima Poinsette. Interview by Peter Wood. Charleston. 3 Feb. 1981. Tape recording.

———. "Literacy and Liberation." *Freedomways: A Quarterly Review of the Negro Freedom Movement* 1.4 (1964): 113–24. Print.

———. Miscellaneous notes on Daufuskie Island. n.d. 30 Jan. 1959. Highlander Library, Highlander Research and Education Center, New Market, TN. Print.

———. Notes on Johns Island. n.d. Box 67, Folder 3. Highlander Research and Education Center Collection. Wisconsin Historical Society, Madison, WI. Print.

———. *Ready from Within: Septima Clark and the Civil Rights Movement.* Ed. Cynthia Stokes Brown. Trenton: Africa World, 1990. Print.

———. "Success of SCLC Citizenship School Seen in 50,000 New Registered Voters." *SCLC Newsletter 1* (1963): n.p. Print.

Clark, Septima Poinsette, with LeGette Blythe. *Echo in My Soul.* New York: Dutton, 1962. Print.

Collins, Patricia Hill. *Black Feminist Thought: Knowledge, Consciousness, and the Politics of Empowerment.* New York: Routledge, 2000. Print.

Cooper, Anna Julia. *A Voice from the South.* New York: Negro Universities P, 1969. Print.

Cornelius, Janet Duitsman. *"When I Can Read My Title Clear": Literacy, Slavery, and Religion in the Antebellum South.* Columbia: U of South Carolina P, 1992. Print.

Cotton, Dorothy. "Citizenship School Report." Records of Southern Christian Leadership Conference, 1954–1970. Martin Luther King, Jr. Library Archives: Atlanta, 1963. Print.

Cushman, Ellen, Eugene R. Kintgen, Barry M. Kroll, and Mike Rose, eds. *Literacy: A Critical Sourcebook.* Boston: Bedford/St. Martin's, 2001. Print.

Davis, Angela Y. *Blues Legacies and Black Feminism: Gertrude "Ma" Rainey, Bessie Smith, and Billie Holiday.* New York: Pantheon, 1998. Print.

———. *Women, Race and Class.* New York: Vintage, 1983. Print.

Duffy, John. *Writing from These Roots: Literacy in a Hmong-American Community.* Honolulu: U of Hawaii P, 2007. Print.

Fallin, Wilson, Jr. *The African American Church in Birmingham, Alabama 1815–1963: A Shelter in the Storm.* New York: Garland, 1997. Print.

Foster, Michelle. *Black Teachers on Teaching.* New York: New, 1997. Print.

Frederick, Marla F. *Between Sundays: Black Women and Everyday Struggles of Faith.* Berkeley: U of California P, 2003. Print.

Freire, Paulo. "The Adult Literacy Process as a Cultural Action for Freedom" and "Education and Conscientização." Cushman, Kintgen, Kroll, and Rose 616–28.

———. *Pedagogy of Freedom: Ethics, Democracy, and Civic Courage.* Lanham: Rowman, 1998. Print.

———. *Pedagogy of the Oppressed.* 1970. New York: Continuum, 2000. Print.

Freire, Paulo, and Donald Macedo. *Literacy: Reading the Word and the World.* Westport: Bergin, 1987. Print.

Fulop, Timothy E., and Albert J. Raboteau, eds. *African-American Religion: Interpretive Essays in History and Culture.* New York: Routledge, 1997. Print.

Gadsden, Sam. *An Oral History of Edisto Island: Sam Gadsden Tells the Story.* Goshen: Pinchpenny, 1975. Print.

Gee, James Paul. *Social Linguistics and Literacies: Ideology in Discourses.* 2nd ed. London: Taylor, 1996. Print.

Gilyard, Keith. "African American Contributions to Composition Studies." *College Composition and Communication* 50.4 (1999): 626–44. Print.

———. "Introduction: Aspects of African American Rhetoric as a Field." Richardson and Jackson 1–20.

Glen, John M. *Highlander, No Ordinary School, 1932–1962.* Lexington: UP of Kentucky, 1988. Print.

Graff, Harvey J. *The Labyrinths of Literacy: Reflections of Literacy Past and Present.* London: Falmer, 1987. Print.

———. *The Literacy Myth: Cultural Integration and Social Structure in the Nineteenth Century.* New Brunswick: Transaction, 1991. Print.

Grimball, Ethel. Interview by Sandra Oldendorf. Charleston. 30 Jan. 1987. Tape recording.

Guttentag, William, and Dan Sturman, dirs. *Soundtrack for a Revolution.* Freedom Song Productions, 2009. DVD.

Gyant, LaVerne. "Contributions of African American Women to Nonformal Education during the Civil Rights Movement, 1955–1965." Diss. Pennsylvania State U, 1990. Print.

Hamlet, Janice D. "Understanding African American Oratory: Manifestations of Nommo." *Afrocentric Visions: Studies in Culture and Communication.* Ed. Janice D. Hamlet. Thousand Oaks: Sage, 1998. 89–107. Print.

Heath, Shirley Brice. *Ways with Words: Language, Life, and Work in Communities and Classrooms.* Cambridge: Cambridge UP, 1983. Print.

Heilbut, Anthony. *The Gospel Sound: Good News and Bad Times.* New York: Simon, 1971. Print.

Herskovits, Melville J. *The Myth of the Negro Past.* Boston: Beacon, 1990. Print.

Highlander Folk School. "Charleston and Sea Island Activities." 1960–61. Box 1, Folder 7. Highlander Research and Education Center Collection. Wisconsin Historical Society, Madison, WI. Print.

———. [Edisto Island Citizenship School Class]. 7 Jan. 1960. Reel 101, Side 1, Part 1. Highlander Research and Education Center Collection. Wisconsin Historical Society, Madison, WI. Tape recording.

———. "Factual Report of Adult School." 1961. Box 38, Folder 4. Highlander Research and Education Center Collection. Wisconsin Historical Society, Madison, WI. Print.

———. "Fiscal Year Report." 1960. Box 1 Folder, 7. Highlander Research and Education Center Collection. Wisconsin Historical Society, Madison, WI. Print.

———. *My Citizenship Booklet.* [Teaching materials]. 1961–62. Box 2, Folder 25 and 26. Highlander Research and Education Center Collection. Wisconsin Historical Society, Madison, WI. Print.

———. *My Reading Booklet 1959–1960* [Teaching materials]. Box 67, Folder 10. Highlander Research and Education Center Collection. Wisconsin Historical Society, Madison, WI. Print.

———. News Release. 4 May 1961. Box 38, Folder 4. Highlander Research and Education Center Collection. Wisconsin Historical Society, Madison, WI. Print.

———. "Notes for Ralph Tyler Memo." 1961b. Box 38, Folder 4. Highlander Research and Education Center Collection. Wisconsin Historical Society, Madison, WI. Print.

———. "A Proposal for the Citizenship School Training Program." Highlander Research and Education Center Collection. N.d. Box 38, File 2. Wisconsin Historical Society, Madison, WI. TS.

———. "Quarterly Report." Winter 1960. Box 2, Folder 25 and 26. Highlander Research and Education Center. New Market, TN. Print.

———. Review of first Citizenship School session. 1957. Tape 515A, Reel 44, Side 1, Part 2. Highlander Research and Education Center Collection. Wisconsin Historical Society, Madison, WI. Tape recording.

———. [Sea Island Reports]. 17 May 1959. Reel 46, Side 1, Part 1. Highlander Research and Education Center Collection. Wisconsin Historical Society, Madison, WI. Tape recording.

———. "Selection of Teachers and Training Leaders for Citizenship Schools." N.d. Box 2, Folder 25 and 26. Highlander Research and Education Center. New Market, TN. TS.

———. "Staff Conference, Monteagle, TN." 31 Jan. 1958. Box 3, Folder 1. Highlander Research and Education Center Collection. Wisconsin Historical Society, Madison, WI. TS.

———. "Statement of Purpose." 3 Apr. 1950. Box 2, Folder 25 and 26. Highlander Research and Education Center. New Market, TN. TS.

Holloway, Joseph. E., ed. *Africanisms in American Culture*. Bloomington: Indiana UP, 1990. Print.

Holt, Thomas. "'Knowledge Is Power': The Black Struggle for Literacy." Lunsford, Moglen, and Slevin 91–102.

Horton, Aimee I. "The Highlander Folk School: A History of the Development of Its Major Programs Related to Social Movements in the South 1932–1961." Diss. U of Chicago, 1971. Print.

———. "Teacher Training Workshop." 1965. Box 2, Folders 25 and 26. Highlander Research and Education Center Collection. Wisconsin Historical Society, Madison, WI. Print.

Horton, Myles, and Paulo Freire. *We Make the Road by Walking: Conversations on Education and Social Change*. Ed. Brenda Bell, John Gaventa, and John Peters. Philadelphia: Temple UP, 1990. Print.

Horton, Myles, and Bill D. Moyers. *Bill Moyers Journal: An Interview with*

Myles Horton: The Adventures of a Radical Hillbilly. New Market: Highlander Research and Education Center, 1983. Print.

Horton, Myles, with Judith Kohl, and Herbert R. Kohl. *The Long Haul: An Autobiography*. New York: Doubleday, 1990. Print.

Hurston, Zora Neale. *Folklore, Memoirs, and Other Writings*. Ed. Cheryl A. Wall. New York: Library of America, 1995. Print.

Jackson, Ronald L. II, and Elaine B. Richardson. *Understanding African American Rhetoric: Classical Origins to Contemporary Innovations*. New York: Routledge, 2003. Print.

Jameson, Fredric. "Cognitive Mapping." *Marxism and the Interpretation of Culture*. Ed. Cary Nelson and Lawrence Grossberg. Urbana: U of Illinois P, 1988. 347–57. Print.

Jenkins, Esau. "Esau Jenkins: Talks." Transcript of tape recording. 1961. Box 16, Folder 10, Tape 515A. Highlander Research and Education Center Collection. Wisconsin Historical Society, Madison, WI. TS.

Johnson, Sarah Coprich. *The Role of the Black Church in Family Literacy*. New York: Lang, 1999. Print.

Kaestle, Carl F., Helen Damon-Moore, Lawrence C. Stedman, Katherine Tinsley, and William Vance Trollinger, Jr. *Literacy in the United States: Readers and Reading since 1880*. New Haven: Yale UP, 1991. Print.

Karenga, Maulana. "Nommo, Kawaida, and Communicative Practice: Bringing Good into the World." Jackson and Richardson 3–22.

Knowles-Borishade, Adetokunbo F. "Paradigm for Classical African Orature: Instrument for a Scientific Revolution?" *Journal of Black Studies* 21.4 (1991): 488–500. Print.

Kynard, Carmen. *Vernacular Insurrections: Race, Black Protest, and the New Century in Composition-Literacies Studies*. Albany: State U of New York P, 2013. Print.

Ladson-Billings, Gloria. "But That's Just Good Teaching! The Case for Culturally Relevant Pedagogy." *Theory Into Practice* 34.3 (1995): 159–65. Print.

———. *The Dreamkeepers: Successful Teachers of African American Children*. San Francisco: Jossey-Bass, 1994. Print.

Levine, David P. "Citizenship Schools." Diss. U of Wisconsin-Madison, 1999. Print.

Levine, Lawrence W. *Black Culture and Black Consciousness: Afro-American Folk Thought from Slavery to Freedom*. New York: Oxford UP, 1977. Print.

Logan, Shirley Wilson. *"We Are Coming": The Persuasive Discourse of Nineteenth-Century Black Women*. Carbondale: Southern Illinois UP, 1999. Print.

———. *With Pen and Voice: A Critical Anthology of Nineteenth-Century African-American Women*. Carbondale: Southern Illinois UP, 1995. Print.

Long, Charles H. "Perspectives for a Study of African-American Religion in the United States." *History of Religion* 11.1 (1971): 54–66. Print.

Lunsford, Andrea A., Helen Moglen, and James Slevin, eds. *The Right to Literacy*. New York: MLA, 1990. Print.

Mack, Anderson. Interview by Rhea Estelle Lathan. Wadmalaw Island, SC. 9 Nov. 2000.

McHenry, Elizabeth. *Forgotten Readers: Recovering the Lost History of African American Literary Societies*. Durham: Duke UP, 2002. Print.

Mintz, Sidney W., and Richard Price. *The Birth of African-American Culture: An Anthropological Perspective*. Boston: Beacon, 1992. Print.

Moody, Joycelyn. *Sentimental Confessions: Spiritual Narratives of Nineteenth-Century African American Women*. Athens: U of Georgia P, 2001. Print.

Morris, Aldon D. *The Origins of the Civil Rights Movement: Black Communities Organizing for Change*. London: Collier-Macmillian, 1984. Print.

Moss, Beverly J. *A Community Text Arises: A Literate Text and a Literacy Tradition in African-American Churches*. Cresskill: Hampton, 2002. Print.

———, ed. *Literacy across Communities*. Cresskill: Hampton, 1994. Print.

Myles Horton, Paulo Freire and Friends Gather at Highlander, 12/5/87. New Market, TN: Highlander Research and Education Center, 1987. Videocassette.

Oldendorf, Sandra Brenneman. "Highlander Folk School and the South Carolina Sea Island Citizenship Schools: Implications for the Social Studies." Diss. U of Kentucky, 1987. Print.

———. "Literacy and Voting: The Story of the South Carolina Sea Island Citizenship Schools." *Education of the African American Adult: An Historical Overview*. Ed. Harvey Neufeldt and Leo McGee. New York: Greenwood, 1990. 191–210. Print.

Parish, Peter J. *Slavery: History and Historians*. New York: Harper, 1989. Print.

———. *Slavery: The Many Faces of a Southern Institution*. Durham: British Association for American Studies, 1979. Print.

Patterson, Orlando. *Freedom in the Making of Western Culture*. New York: Basic, 1991. Print.

Payne, Charles M. *I've Got the Light of Freedom: The Organizing Tradition and the Mississippi Freedom Struggle*. Berkeley: U of California P, 1996. Print.

Prendergast, Catherine. *Literacy and Racial Justice: The Politics of Learning after Brown v. Board of Education*. Carbondale: Southern Illinois UP, 2003. Print.

———. "Race: The Absent Presence in Composition Studies." *College Composition and Communication* 50.1 (1998): 36–53. Print.

Rachal, John R. "Gideonites and Freedmen: Adult Literacy Education at Port Royal, 1862–1866." *Journal of Negro Education* 55.4 (1986): 453–69. Print.

Reagon, Bernice Johnson. *If You Don't Go, Don't Hinder Me: The African American Sacred Song Tradition*. Lincoln: U of Nebraska P, 2001. Print.

———, ed. *We'll Understand It Better By and By: Pioneering African American Gospel Composers*. Washington: Smithsonian Institution, 1992. Print.

———, prod. and comp. *Voices of the Civil Rights Movement: Black American Freedom Songs 1960–1966*. [Various Artists]. Smithsonian Folkways Recordings, 1980. CD and Print.

Richardson, Elaine. *African American Literacies*. New York: Routledge, 2003. Print.

Richardson, Elaine B., and Ronald L. Jackson II, eds. *African American Rhetoric(s): Interdisciplinary Perspectives*. Carbondale: Southern Illinois UP, 2004. Print.

Robinson, Bernice. Interview by Sandra Brenneman Oldendorf. 15 Jan. 1986. Box 1, Folder 5. Bernice Robinson Collection. Avery Research Center, Charleston, SC.

——— Interview by Sue Thrasher and Eliot Wigginton. 9 Nov. 1980. Box 1, Folder 5. Bernice Robinson Collection. Avery Research Center, Charleston, SC.

Robinson, Jo Ann Gibson. *The Montgomery Bus Boycott and the Women Who Started It: The Memoir of Jo Ann Gibson Robinson*. Ed. David J. Garrow. Knoxville: U of Tennessee P, 1987. Print.

Ross, Rosetta E. *Witnessing and Testifying: Black Women, Religion, and Civil Rights*. Minneapolis: Fortress, 2003. Print.

Royster, Jacqueline Jones. "Perspectives on the Intellectual Tradition of Black Women Writers." Lunsford, Moglen, and Slevin 103–19.

———. "To Call a Thing by Its True Name: The Rhetoric of Ida B. Wells." *Reclaiming Rhetorica: Women in the Rhetorical Tradition*. Ed. Andrea A. Lunsford. Pittsburgh: U of Pittsburgh P, 1995. 167–84. Print.

———. *Traces of a Stream: Literacy and Social Change among African American Women*. Pittsburgh: U of Pittsburgh P, 2000. Print.

———. "When the First Voice You Hear Is Not Your Own." *College Composition and Communication* 47.1 (1996): 29–40. Print.

Royster, Jacqueline Jones, and Jean C. Williams. "History in the Spaces Left: African American Presence and Narratives of Composition Studies." *College Composition and Communication* 50.4 (1999): 563–84. Print.

Scribner, Sylvia, and Michael Cole. *The Psychology of Literacy.* Cambridge: Harvard UP, 1981. Print.

Second Step Voter Education Schools, 1963–65. Box 68, Folder 1 and 6. Highlander Research and Education Center Collection. Wisconsin Historical Society, Madison, WI. Print.

Smith, Barbara. *The Truth That Never Hurts: Writings on Race, Gender, and Freedom.* New Brunswick, NJ: Rutgers UP, 1998. Print.

Smitherman, Geneva. *Talkin' and Testifyin': The Language of Black America.* Detroit: Wayne State UP, 1986. Print.

———. *Talkin' That Talk: Language, Culture, and Education in African America.* New York: Routledge, 2000. Print.

———. *Word from the Mother: Language and African Americans.* New York: Routledge, 2006. Print.

Stepto, Robert B. *From Behind the Veil: A Study of Afro-American Narrative.* 2nd ed. Urbana: U of Illinois P, 1991. Print.

Street, Brian V. "The New Literacy Studies." Cushman, Kintgen, Kroll, and Rose 431–42.

———. "Recent Applications of New Literacy Studies in Educational Contexts." *Research in the Teaching of English* 39.4 (2005): 417–23. Print.

Strickland, Donna. *The Managerial Unconscious in the History of Composition Studies.* Carbondale: Southern Illinois UP, 2011. Print.

Thompson, Robert Farris. *Flash of the Spirit: African and Afro-American Art and Philosophy.* New York: Random, 1983. Print.

Tjerandsen, Carl. *Education for Citizenship: A Foundation's Experience.* Santa Cruz: Emil Schwarzhaupt Foundation, 1980. Print.

Tyson, Timothy B. *Radio Free Dixie: Robert F. Williams and the Roots of Black Power.* Chapel Hill: U of North Carolina P, 1999. Print.

Werner, Craig Hansen. *A Change Is Gonna Come: Music, Race & the Soul of America.* New York: Plume, 1998. Print.

———. *Higher Ground: Stevie Wonder, Aretha Franklin, Curtis Mayfield, and the Rise and Fall of American Soul.* New York: Crown, 2004. Print.

———. *Playing the Changes: From Afro-Modernism to the Jazz Impulse.* Urbana: U of Illinois P, 1994. Print.

White, Deborah Gray. *Too Heavy a Load: Black Women in Defense of Themselves, 1894–1994.* New York: Norton, 1999. Print.

Wigginton, Eliot. *Refuse to Stand Silently By: An Oral History of Grass Roots Social Activism in America, 1921–1964.* New York: Doubleday, 1991. Print.

Williams, Heather Andrea. *Self-Taught: African American Education in Slavery and Freedom.* Chapel Hill: U of North Carolina P, 2007. Print.

Williams, Kimmika L. H. "Ties That Bind: A Comparative Analysis of Zora Neale Hurston's and Geneva Smitherman's Work." Richardson and Jackson 86–107.

Williams-Jones, Pearl. "Afro-American Gospel Music: A Crystallization of the Black Aesthetic." *Ethnomusicology* 19.3 (1975): 373–85. Print.

Woodson, Carter Godwin. *The Mis-education of the Negro.* New York: AMS, 1977. Print.

———. "Proceedings of the Annual Meeting of the Association for the Study of Negro Life and History Held in New York City. November 8–12, 1932." *Journal of Negro History* 17.1 (1933): 1–7. Print

Woodyard, Jeffrey Lynn. "Africological Theory and Criticism: Reconceptualizing Communication Constructs." Jackson and Richardson 133–54.

Young, Andrew. *An Easy Burden: The Civil Rights Movement and the Transformation of America.* New York: Harper, 1996. Print.

INDEX

Acknowledging the burden, xvii–xviii,
16–18, 26–43
at Citizenship Schools, historical
overview of, 29–33, 35–41
combination of history and power
in, 16–17
empowering nature of, 17, 30
literacy activism and, 27–28, 31–32
segregation and, 26–29, 31
Adams, F., 39, 40, 42, 52
Afrafeminism, 4
Alkebulin, A. A., 16
American Missionary Association
(AMA), 117
Anderson, J. D., xxiii, 114
Andrews, W., 65, 119
Asante, M., 115

Banks, A., xxiii
Bearing witness, xviii, 18–23, 74,
75–76, 79–80, 82–96, 97–104,
111, 120
classroom example of, 97–104
definition of, 18–19
group experience and, 79
in instructional methods, 82–96
in literacy learning curriculum, 19,
74, 78
as means of inspiring, 111
placing in larger context, 75–76,
79–80, 86
spiritual element of, 21
in teacher training program, 85–86
Belafonte, H., 26, 29

Besnier, N., 114
Boles, J. B., 114
Bond, J., 43
Boulware, M. H., 113
Brandt, D., xxii, xxiii, 11, 113
Brewer, A., xix, xx, 82, 83–84, 96,
97–104, 108
classroom instruction example of,
97–104
Brotherhood of Sleeping Car Porters,
29
Brown, S., 67, 123
Brown v. Board of Education of Topeka,
xiii, 28–29
validation of African Americans by,
29
Butler, J., 114

Cabrillo Community College Literacy
Conference, 55
Call-and-response, xviii, 8–16, 46,
51–52, 56
African origins of, 8
in Civil Rights Movement, 11, 16
as communication strategy, 8–9
definitions of, 8–9, 12
in establishment of Citizenship
Schools, 46, 51–52
as intellectual activity, 16
leader role in, 51–52
in literacy practice, 9
as organizing principle in African
American culture, 13
participatory nature of, 10

AUTHOR

 **Rhea Estelle Lathan** is an assistant professor of English rhetoric and composition at Florida State University. She teaches and writes about cultural literacy, language, and critical race theory, as well as community-based African American literacy activism.

This book was typeset in Garamond and Frutiger by Barbara Frazier.
Typefaces used on the cover include Adobe Garamond and Formata.
The book was printed on 55-lb. Natural Offset paper
by King Printing Company, Inc.